C
12.6.08

CCNA Video Mentor

Second Edition

Wendell Odom, CCIE® No. 1624

Cisco Press

800 East 96th Street

Indianapolis, Indiana 46240 USA

CCNA Video Mentor

Second Edition

Wendell Odom

Copyright® 2008 Cisco Systems, Inc.

Published by:
Cisco Press
800 East 96th Street
Indianapolis, IN 46240 USA

Printed in the United States of America

First Printing December 2007

Library of Congress Cataloging-in-Publication Data is on file.

ISBN-13: 978-1-58720-191-2

ISBN-10: 1-58720-191-7

Publisher
Paul Boger

Associate Publisher
Dave Dusthimer

Cisco Representative
Anthony Wolfenden

Cisco Press Program Manager
Jeff Brady

Executive Editor
Brett Bartow

Managing Editor
Patrick Kanouse

Senior Development Editor
Christopher A. Cleveland

Senior Project Editor
Tonya Simpson

Technical Editor
Stephen Kalman

Editorial Assistant
Vanessa Evans

Book Designer
Louisa Adair

Composition
Mark Shirar

Proofreader
Jennifer Gallant

Warning and Disclaimer

Feedback Information

At Cisco Press, our goal is to create in-depth technical books of the highest quality and value. Each book is crafted with care and precision, undergoing rigorous development that involves the unique expertise of members from the professional technical community.

Readers' feedback is a natural continuation of this process. If you have any comments regarding how we could improve the quality of this book, or otherwise alter it to better suit your needs, you can contact us through email at feedback@ciscopress.com. Please make sure to include the book title and ISBN in your message.

We greatly appreciate your assistance.

Trademark Acknowledgments

All terms mentioned in this book that are known to be trademarks or service marks have been appropriately capitalized. Cisco Press or Cisco Systems, Inc. cannot attest to the accuracy of this information. Use of a term in this book should not be regarded as affecting the validity of any trademark or service mark.

Corporate and Government Sales

The publisher offers excellent discounts on this book when ordered in quantity for bulk purchases or special sales, which may include electronic versions and/or custom covers and content particular to your business, training goals, marketing focus, and branding interests. For more information, please contact:

U.S. Corporate and Government Sales   1-800-382-3419   corpsales@pearsontechgroup.com

For sales outside the United States please contact:
International Sales   international@pearsoned.com

Americas Headquarters	Asia Pacific Headquarters	Europe Headquarters
Cisco Systems, Inc.	Cisco Systems, Inc.	Cisco Systems International BV
170 West Tasman Drive	168 Robinson Road	Haarlerbergpark
San Jose, CA 95134-1706	#28-01 Capital Tower	Haarlerbergweg 13-19
USA	Singapore 068912	1101 CH Amsterdam
www.cisco.com	www.cisco.com	The Netherlands
Tel: 408 526-4000	Tel: +65 6317 7777	www-europe.cisco.com
800 553-NETS (6387)	Fax: +65 6317 7799	Tel: +31 0 800 020 0791
Fax: 408 527-0883		Fax: +31 0 20 357 1100

Cisco has more than 200 offices worldwide. Addresses, phone numbers, and fax numbers are listed on the Cisco Website at **www.cisco.com/go/offices.**

About the Author

Wendell Odom, CCIE No. 1624, splits time between writing Cisco Press books and teaching Cisco authorized training for Skyline Advanced Technology Services (http://www.skyline-ats.com). Wendell has worked in the networking arena for more than 25 years, with jobs in pre- and post-sales technical consulting, teaching, and course development. He is the author of all prior editions of the Cisco Press *CCNA Exam Certification Guides*, most recently the two-book set *CCENT/CCNA ICND1 Official Exam Certification Guide* and *CCNA ICND2 Official Exam Certification Guide*. Wendell has also authored several other titles, including the *CCIE Routing/Switching Written Exam Certification Guide*, *QoS Exam Certification Guide*, and *Computer Networking First-Step*, all from Cisco Press.

About the Technical Reviewer

Stephen Kalman is a data security trainer and the author or technical editor of more than 20 books, courses, and CBT titles. His most recent book is *Web Security Field Guide*, published by Cisco Press. In addition to those responsibilities he runs a consulting company, Esquire Micro Consultants, which specializes in network security assessments and forensics.

Mr. Kalman holds SSCP, CISSP, ISSMP, ISSAP, CEH, CHFI, CCNA, CCSA (Checkpoint), A+, Network+, and Security+ certifications and is a member of the New York State Bar.

Dedications

For Hannah Grace: Thanks for all the help learning how to draw on the computer.

Acknowledgments

I imagine Steve Kalman, my tech editor on yet another project, might need a break—we've worked on a lot of projects together in the last year or two. Thankfully, Steve never seems to tire in helping me with the books and with these videos. Steve did his usual wonderful job of looking at the little details while also looking out for the bigger picture, helping make this product better. Steve, thanks again for all the good work!

Chris Cleveland got the wonderful opportunity (tee hee) to listen to all the videos, even the old ones that Chris had already listened to a dozen times last year. Chris was great at finding every last little picky thing that could be changed in each video, but then helping me pick which ones made sense to change, with a lot of thinking outside the box. Chris, many thanks for the usual wonderful job, and no, you weren't being too picky!

Eric Strom played several roles with this product, from recording and editing the live video sections, to creating the product menus and putting the finishing touches on the video/audio itself. The Cisco Press Video Mentor series owes a lot to the efforts, skills, and knowledge supplied by Eric—thanks much!

As usual, a lot of people have a hand in taking what I submit and causing it to magically appear as a product—a group we generally call "the production folks." Thanks for making my products shine as much as they can!

Thanks to Jeff Doyle for the heads-up on the Rode Podcaster microphone I used for all the new videos—excellent suggestion!

Brett Bartow did his usual wonderful job in talking me through the product from the big-picture perspective, helping determine the organization, size, timing, positioning, and essentially anything to help make the product successful. And he writes our decisions down, so when I forget some of the choices we made after being down in the trenches for a few weeks, he can set me back on the straight and narrow. Thanks, Brett, for keeping our little juggling act in the air.

Finally, on a personal note, thanks to wife Kris and daughter Hannah for giving up a few games of chasing around the kitchen when I was recording. I promise to find a way to integrate into the audio track some of the sounds of you two running over my head playing chase in the house. And as always, I'd like to thank Jesus Christ for caring about every part of our lives, including the work and effort spent making these videos.

Contents at a Glance

Contents

ICND1 Labs

ICND2 Labs

Icons Used in This Book

Command Syntax Conventions

The conventions used to present command syntax in this book are the same conventions used in the IOS Command Reference. The Command Reference describes these conventions as follows:

- **Boldface** indicates commands and keywords that are entered literally as shown. In actual configuration examples and output (not general command syntax), boldface indicates commands that are manually input by the user (such as a **show** command).

- *Italics* indicate arguments for which you supply actual values.

- Vertical bars (l) separate alternative, mutually exclusive elements.

- Square brackets [ ] indicate optional elements.

- Braces { } indicate a required choice.

- Braces within brackets [{ }] indicate a required choice within an optional element.

Introduction

The *CCNA Video Mentor*, Second Edition (CVM), helps both CCENT and CCNA candidates prepare to pass the ICND1, ICND2, and CCNA exams by supplying 20 instructional videos covering core CCNA exam topics. Each CVM video presents a unique lab scenario, with both visual references and audio explanations of what you should expect to happen in each lab. Most of the videos also show the details of the command-line interface (CLI) commands used to implement the features described in each lab video, along with running commentary. The end result is a set of videos that explain some of the most important CCNA topics, providing you with thorough explanations from a trusted mentor.

This product is one of several products in the Cisco Press Video Mentor series. The Video Mentor series—created because of many requests from Cisco Press book readers—provides something more than just the static written word of a typical book. Many people learn better in a classroom setting, with an instructor explaining the concepts while showing details projected on the wall. This product, along with the other products in the Video Mentor series, provides a product closer to what you might get in a class.

Who Should Use the *CCNA Video Mentor*?

The *CCNA Video Mentor* is primarily intended for people using self-study books as their primary method of preparing to pass the Cisco ICND1, ICND2, and CCNA exams. Additionally, this product should be useful to anyone who is studying basic networking topics, either by reading books or by taking classes.

Goals and Methods

CCNA Video Mentor, Second Edition, has a very specific set of goals. First, these videos help you more completely and thoroughly understand several of the most important CCENT and CCNA exam topics. Although you might have already read about these topics in other books or heard about them in classes, *CCNA Video Mentor* helps you master these particular topics. Using these videos in addition to reading a book or attending a course helps solidify your knowledge and helps you see how to apply the knowledge to better prepare you for the application of that knowledge on the exam.

Note that *CCNA Video Mentor* does not attempt to cover all possible topics on the exams used to achieve CCENT and CCNA certification. It is intended to be used to supplement both self-study efforts and classroom training.

The *CCNA Video Mentor's* video labs show the activity on a computer desktop with a running audio commentary from the author. Most of the videos follow the same basic approach, using these steps:

1. The video begins with a description of the goals of the video.

2. The lab scenario steps (usually two or three steps) are listed, giving a general outline of what the viewer should expect to see and hear during the video.

3. The network topology used in the video is described.

4. Then, for each scenario step:

    a) The video shows what the user should expect from the particular part of the lab exercise.

    b) The video shows the CLI details of how to configure and verify that the routers and switches are working properly.

Some of the subnetting videos do not have a CLI component because these videos focus on concepts and processes instead of configuration.

A Brief Word About the Related Exams

This product helps you prepare to achieve a CCNA certification. Two paths exists via which you can become CCNA certified:

- Take the CCNA exam (640-802)
- Take both the ICND1 exam (640-822) and the ICND2 exam (640-816)

Because you might be using the two-exam approach, the videos have been organized based on whether the content is most likely to be seen in the ICND1 exam or the ICND2 exam. All the content could be assessed as part of the 640-802 CCNA exam.

This product also helps you prepare to achieve CCENT certification. Cisco awards a CCENT certification for those passing the ICND1 (640-822) exam.

CVM Contents

The CVM product package contains two components: a DVD and a booklet. The DVD contains the 20 lab videos, plus several introductory videos. The DVD has been optimized for viewing on a computer, with a 1024 × 768 minimum pixel grid.

The booklet lists reference information that can be useful when watching the videos; the booklet is not intended as a standalone tool. The booklet has a section corresponding to each of the 20 CVM video labs, with each section containing a copy of the figures and other material shown in the video. Each section includes the following:

- The list of objectives for the video
- The list of scenario steps
- Copies of all figures shown in the video
- Copies of all reference lists shown in the video
- The beginning configuration on each device
- Any configuration added to each device during the video

How the *CCNA Video Mentor* Is Organized

When the DVD starts, the application displays a menu that lists the two major parts of the product: labs related to the ICND1 exam and labs related to the ICND2 exam. A video introducing the entire product is also available from this initial menu.

Clicking either the ICND1 or ICND2 items moves the user to one of two submenus. Each submenu lists a set of videos, organized into various topics. These submenus also supply clickable links to see an introductory video for each general topic area, plus links to display a PDF for the booklet chapter for each individual lab.

The printed booklet mimics the organization of the labs in the DVD application, organizing the labs into two major groups (ICND1 and ICND2), and smaller topical groupings as well. The groups and labs associated with the ICND1 exam are as follows:

Part I: CLI Basics

- **Lab 1, "Navigating Router/Switch Command-Line Interface"**—This lab demonstrates how to connect to a router or switch console and use both user mode and privileged mode exec commands.

- **Lab 2, "Router Configuration and Managing Configuration Files"**—This lab leads the user through the process of connecting to a router's console, getting into configuration mode, and configuring several features. It also explains the key commands used for copying configuration files.

Part II: LANs

- **Lab 3, "Switching Basics: Learning, Forwarding/Filtering, and Interface Settings"**— This lab shows a sample network with two LAN switches and explains how the switches will learn and forward certain frames. It also shows the MAC address learning process with **show** commands on the switches, along with some basic interface configuration subcommands on switches.

Part III: IP Addressing and Subnetting

- **Lab 4, "Finding the Subnet Number"**—This lab shows how to find the subnet number in which an IP address resides. It emphasizes the use of a process shown in the Cisco Press Exam Certification Guides, a process which shows how to find the answers to subnetting questions without using any binary math.

- **Lab 5, "Finding the Broadcast Address and Range of Addresses in a Subnet"**—This lab shows how to find a subnet's broadcast address and the range of valid addresses in the subnet given the subnet number. This video lab continues the same problem shown in ICND1 video lab 4, again using a decimal-only process from the Cisco Press Exam Certification Guides.

- **Lab 6, "Finding All Subnets of a Network with Less than 8 Subnet Bits"**—This lab shows how to find all the subnet numbers of a single classful network, assuming a single subnet mask is used throughout the classful network. This video emphasizes the use of yet another decimal-only process shown in the Cisco Press Exam Certification Guides. This video uses the same network and subnet mask used in labs 4 and 5.

- **Lab 7, "IP Subnet Design and Implementation"**—This lab explains subnetting from a design perspective, examining how to determine the number of required subnets and reviewing how to find all subnets of a network using a particular static-length mask.

Part IV: Routing and Routing Protocols

- **Lab 8, "Static and Connected Routes"**—This lab explains the concept of the details of an IP routing table on a Cisco router. It then shows the requirements for a router to add connected routes to its routing table, as well as how to configure two different styles of static routes.

- **Lab 9, "RIP Configuration"**—This lab shows how to configure RIP in a simple three-router WAN. It focuses on the meaning of the RIP **network** configuration subcommand; in particular, how the **network** command matches a router's interfaces, and what the router does when the **network** command matches an interface. It also explains the default version settings when the **version** command is not configured, and shows how to configure RIP Version 2.

The groups and labs associated with the ICND2 exam are as follows:

Part I: LANs

- **Lab 1, "Configuring VLANs"**—This lab shows two variations of how to configure VLANs on a switch. The lab shows how to configure a VLAN, as well as how to place interfaces into that particular VLAN.

- **Lab 2, "VTP Servers and Clients"**—This lab shows how to configure both VTP servers and VTP clients so that when VLANs are configured on the server, the client dynamically learns about the VLAN. This lab focuses on how to determine whether two neighboring switches meet all the requirements for them to be able to successfully exchange VLAN information.

Part II: Routing Protocols

- **Lab 3, "RIP with Split Horizon, Route Poisoning, and Poison Reverse"**—This lab explains the concepts behind some of the more advanced distance vector loop avoidance features. It also demonstrates these features in a small network using the output of IOS **debug** commands.

- **Lab 4, "Single Area and Multi-area OSPF Configuration"**—This lab shows how to configure OSPF in a five-router WAN. It shows how to configure OSPF as simply as possible, using a single OSPF area, as well as how to configure Area Border Routers (ABR) in a multi-area design.

- **Lab 5, "EIGRP Configuration and Operation"**—This lab shows how to configure EIGRP in a simple three-router WAN. It focuses on the meaning of the EIGRP **network** configuration subcommand; in particular, how the wildcard mask option allows an engineer to control on which interfaces the router enables EIGRP. It also shows the contents of the IP routing table when Variable Length Subnet Masking (VLSM) is used.

- **Lab 6, "Understanding EIGRP Metric Calculations"**—This lab shows how EIGRP calculates its integer metric value based on interface bandwidth and delay. It also shows examples of the metric from the CLI, as well as how to influence the calculated metric—and therefore the routes chosen by EIGRP—by tuning the interface bandwidth.

Part III: Scaling IP Addresses

- **Lab 7, "NAT Overload (PAT)"**—This lab explains how the NAT overload feature (also known as PAT) works, and how it allows the use of a small number of public IP addresses to support a large network. The lab also reviews the NAT overload configuration for a sample network.

- **Lab 8, "IPv6 Subnetting and Address Configuration"**—This lab shows the format of IPv6 global unicast addresses, along with a comparison of how to subnet IPv4 and IPv6 global unicast addresses. The lab also shows how to configure IPv6 addresses on a Cisco router.

Part IV: WAN

■ **Lab 9, "PPP and CHAP Configuration"**—This lab explains the two interface status codes and the impact of both correct and incorrect WAN data link configuration parameters. The lab also shows how to configure PPP and CHAP on a serial link.

Part V: Security

■ **Lab 10, "Access Lists"**—This lab explains the syntax of the **access-list** command for configuring an extended IP ACL. The video focuses on how to match ranges of IP addresses using a wildcard mask, as well as matching the well-known port number as a destination port.

■ **Lab 11, "Access Lists II"**—This lab explains the nuances of matching well-known ports as the source port in an **access-list** command by showing an alternative solution for the scenario described in Lab 10. This video shows how to filter packets going from a server to a client by matching the source port of a packet.

Suggested Times to Use Labs

The *CCNA Video Mentor*, Second Edition, supplements the learning process using CCNA self-study products. The following table suggests the points at which each CVM lab might be best used in conjunction with the Cisco Press CCNA books.

Table I-1 shows the best timing options when using the *CCNA Official Exam Certification Library*, Third Edition (978-1-58720-183-7), which consists of the *CCENT/CCNA ICND1 Official Exam Certification Guide* and the *CCNA ICND2 Official Exam Certification Guide*.

Table I-1   Using the CVM with the Official CCNA Certification Library

ICND1 Labs

Lab	Book	Chapter(s)
1	ICND1 ECG	8, 13
2	ICND1 ECG	13
3	ICND1 ECG	9
4	ICND1 ECG	12
5	ICND1 ECG	12
6	ICND1 ECG	12
7	ICND1 ECG	12
8	ICND1 ECG	14
9	ICND1 ECG	14

ICND2 Labs

Lab	Book	Chapter(s)
1	ICND2 ECG	1
2	ICND2 ECG	1
3	ICND2 ECG	8
4	ICND2 ECG	9
5	ICND2 ECG	10
6	ICND2 ECG	10
7	ICND2 ECG	16
8	ICND2 ECG	17
9	ICND2 ECG	12
10	ICND2 ECG	6
11	ICND2 ECG	6

The CCNA certification can be achieved through two different paths: by taking the single CCNA (640-802) exam or by taking both the ICND1 (640-822) and ICND2 (640-816) exams. This product separates the video labs into two sections, with labs focusing on the ICND1 exam in this section and labs focusing on the ICND2 exam in the other section. The labs in both sections apply to the CCNA exam.

Part I   CLI Basics

Lab 1   Navigating Router/Switch Command-Line Interface

Lab 2   Router Configuration and Managing Configuration Files

Part II   LANs

Lab 3   Switch Basics: Learning, Forwarding/Filtering, and Interface Settings

Part III   IP Addressing and Subnetting

Lab 4   Finding the Subnet Number

Lab 5   Finding the Broadcast Address and Range of Addresses in a Subnet

Lab 6   Finding All Subnets of a Network with Fewer Than 8 Subnet Bits

Lab 7   IP Subnet Design and Implementation

Part IV   Routing and Routing Protocols

Lab 8   Static and Connected Routes

Lab 9   RIP Configuration

Navigating a Router/Switch Command-Line Interface

This *CCNA Video Mentor* (CVM) lab covers the most basic skills for accessing and using the command-line interface (CLI) on a Cisco router or switch. Many of the small, picky details of how the CLI works cannot be seen by reading a book; this lab hopes to complete the coverage of those basics. In particular, the objectives of this lab are as follows:

- Use IOS CLI help features

- Describe the differences between user, enable, and config modes

- Describe the difference between EXEC commands and configuration commands

- Move among user, enable, and configuration modes

Scenario

This lab contains two main steps. The first step focuses on the basics of the CLI, and the second step examines different CLI modes and how to move between them. The video takes the following actions at the two steps:

Step 1. From the console port, the user logs in to a router and experiments with user EXEC mode. This step shows how to get command-line help.

Step 2. The user moves among user EXEC mode, privileged (enable) EXEC mode, and configuration mode. This step demonstrates some commands that might be allowed only in a particular mode.

Initial Configurations

Many labs in the CVIP have meaningful initial configurations. If you use this lab at the suggested point in your study, you will not yet have seen some of the configurations. However, for completeness, Example 1-1 shows the initial configuration of router R1 at the beginning of the lab. The parts of R1's configuration that are not relevant to this lab have been omitted.

Example 1-1   Initial Configuration for R1

```
hostname R1
```

Ending Configurations

This lab ends with the configuration unchanged.

Video Presentation Reference

The video presents figures, tables, and text with short lectures before showing the CLI of the router. This section simply lists these figures and tables for reference.

Figure 1-1 shows a diagram of the network used in this example.

Figure 1-1   Lab 1 Network Topology

Because the video is organized into two separate steps, the reference materials have been organized into two separate sections.

Step 1 Reference

Figure 1-2   Figure for Step 1

- User EXEC Mode Facts:
  - <u>First</u> mode seen by users connected from the console port, aux port, and Telnet.
  - User can type <u>harmless</u> EXEC commands.
  - Characterized by a ">" at the end of the command prompt.

Step 2 Reference

Figure 1-3 **Figure for Step 2**

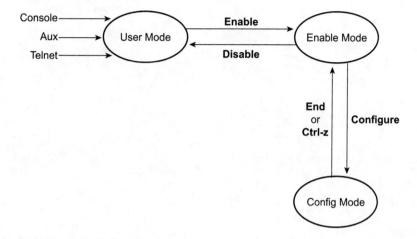

Table 1-1 **Comparing EXEC and Config Commands**

	EXEC Commands	Config Commands
Mode in which they are used	User or enable	Config
Cisco IOS Software typically responds with a list of messages	Yes	No
Command changes the configuration and behavior of router/switch	No	Yes

Table 1-2 **Three Commands That Can Be Used in Different CLI Modes**

Command	Modes in Which It Works
show ip route	User, enable
reload	Enable
hostname	Config

Router Configuration and Managing Configuration Files

This *CCNA Video Mentor* lab demonstrates the mechanics of configuring a Cisco router and how to copy configuration files. The objectives of this lab are the following:

- Describe the configuration process using different configuration modes

- Recognize the *command prompts* seen in different configuration modes

- Copy configuration files using the **copy** command

Scenario

This lab contains two primary steps. The first step focuses on an example of moving around in configuration mode, with the goal of explaining the process rather than the specific commands. The second step focuses on how to copy configuration files on a Cisco router. The video references these two main steps as follows:

Step 1. Using configuration mode

Step 2. Viewing and copying configuration files in NVRAM, RAM, and TFTP servers

Initial Configurations

The only router shown in this video begins with almost no configuration other than a host name. Example 2-1 lists the hostname configuration for reference.

Example 2-1   Initial Configuration for Router R1

```
hostname R1
```

Ending Configurations

By the end of the lab, R1's running and startup configuration files should be identical. The video also shows a couple of other configuration items. Example 2-2 lists the ending configuration after all steps in the lab.

Example 2-2   Ending Configuration for R1

```
hostname Fred
!
interface serial 0/1/0
 ip address 1.1.1.1 255.255.255.0
!
line con 0
 password cisco
 login
```

Video Presentation Reference

The video presents figures, tables, and text with short lectures before showing the CLI of the router. This section simply lists these figures and tables for reference. Figure 2-1 shows a diagram of the network used in this example.

Figure 2-1   Lab 2 Network Topology

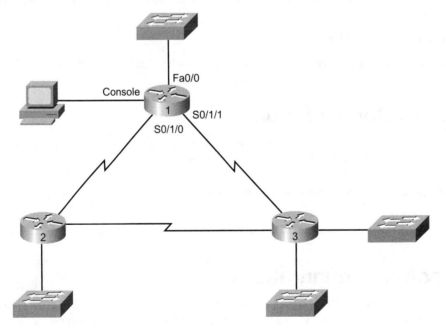

Because the video is organized into two separate steps, the reference materials have been organized into two separate sections.

Step 1 Reference

Figure 2-2   **Accessing a Router's Config Mode**

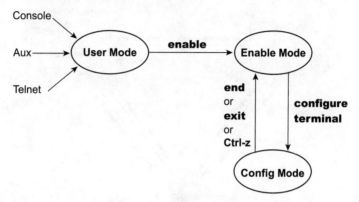

Table 2-1   **Example Configuration Sub-modes**

Name of Sub-mode	Purpose	Command Prompt
Interface	Configures details about a specific router interface, such as the IP address	Router(config-if)#
Line	Configures details about lines (console, vty, and aux)	Router(config-line)#
Router	Configures details about a particular routing protocol	Router(config-router)#

Step 2 Reference

Figure 2-3   Mechanics of the copy Command

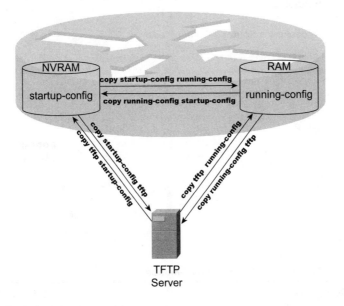

Switch Basics: Learning, Forwarding/Filtering, and Interface Settings

This *CCNA Video Mentor* lab reviews the logic of how switches learn entries for their MAC address tables and make forwarding and filtering decisions based on those tables; it also shows some of the most basic configuration settings on a Cisco LAN switch. In particular, the objectives of this lab are as follows:

- Predict the types of entries to be found in a switch's *MAC address table*
- Describe how switches make forwarding/filtering decisions
- Configure the following:
  - Interface speed and duplex settings
  - Switch IP address and default gateway

Scenario

This lab contains two main steps, as follows:

Step 1. Observe the addition of new MAC address table entries

Step 2. Configure basic settings:
- Interface speed and duplex
- IP address and default gateway

Initial Configurations

The two switches in this lab begin with very little configuration—each switch simply has a hostname configured. Examples 3-1 and 3-2 list the hostname configurations for completeness.

Example 3-1   Initial Configuration for Sw1

```
hostname Sw1
```

Example 3-2   Initial Configuration for Sw2

```
hostname Sw2
```

Ending Configurations

This lab adds some configuration commands to both Sw1 and Sw2. Examples 3-3 and 3-4 show the configuration added during the lab.

Example 3-3   Configuration on Sw1 Added During This Lab

```
enable secret cisco
!
interface FastEthernet 0/23
 duplex full
 speed 100
!
interface vlan 1
  ip address 172.30.1.101 255.255.255.0
 !
ip default-gateway 172.30.1.251
 !
```

Example 3-4   Configuration on Sw2 Added During This Lab

```
interface FastEthernet 0/24
 duplex full
 speed 100

 !
interface vlan 1
  ip address 172.30.1.102 255.255.255.0
 !
ip default-gateway 172.30.1.251
```

Video Presentation Reference

This video presents several figures and a table that support the concepts covered in the lab. This section simply lists these figures for reference. Because the video is organized into two separate steps, the reference materials have been organized into two separate sections.

Step 1 Reference

Figure 3-1   Completed MAC Address Tables After Learning All PC MAC Addresses

Sw1 MAC Address Table

Address	Interface
0033.3333.3333	Fa0/13
0011.1111.1111	Fa0/11
0022.2222.2222	Fa0/23

Sw2 MAC Address Table

Address	Interface
0033.3333.3333	Fa0/24
0011.1111.1111	Fa0/24
0022.2222.2222	Fa0/12

Figure 3-2   Forwarding Path and MAC Address Table Entries Used for Frames from PC3 to PC1

Sw1 MAC Address Table

Address	Interface
0033.3333.3333	Fa0/13
0011.1111.1111	Fa0/11
0022.2222.2222	Fa0/23

Sw2 MAC Address Table

Address	Interface
0033.3333.3333	Fa0/24
0011.1111.1111	Fa0/24
0022.2222.2222	Fa0/12

Figure 3-3   Forwarding Path and MAC Address Table Entries Used for Frames from PC3 to PC2

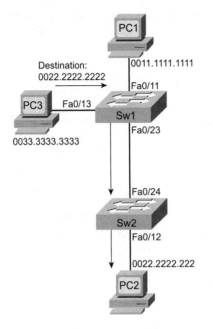

Sw1 MAC Address Table

Address	Interface
0033.3333.3333	Fa0/13
0011.1111.1111	Fa0/11
0022.2222.2222	Fa0/23

Sw2 MAC Address Table

Address	Interface
0033.3333.3333	Fa0/24
0011.1111.1111	Fa0/24
0022.2222.2222	Fa0/12

Step 2 Reference

Table 3-1   Switch Configuration Command Reference

Command	Purpose
interface fastethernet *x/y*	Moves the user into interface configuration mode
speed {10 | 100}	Manually sets the speed of the interface
duplex {half | full}	Manually sets the duplex of an interface
interface vlan 1	Moves the user to VLAN 1 configuration mode
ip address *address mask*	Allows the configuration of a management IP address on the switch
ip default-gateway *address*	Defines the switch's default gateway IP address

Figure 3-4   IP Address Reference

Finding the Subnet Number

This *CCNA Video Mentor* (CVM) lab explains how to find the subnet number in which an IP address resides. In particular, it shows you how to find the subnet number in which 128.200.100.100, mask 255.255.224.0, resides.

The objectives of this lab are as follows:

- To help you understand how to use a particular process (found in the Cisco Press *CCENT/CCNA ICND1 Official Exam Certification Guide*) to find an address's resident subnet

- To help you understand how to find the answers to this kind of question quickly, accurately, and with confidence

Scenario

This lab contains a single step, focusing on the process by which to find the subnet number (128.200.96.0/19) in which IP address 128.200.100.100/19 resides.

Video Presentation Reference

The video presents figures, tables, and text with short lectures before showing the command-line interface (CLI) of the router. This section simply lists these figures and tables for reference.

Figure 4-1 shows the part of an internetwork in which IP address 128.200.100.100/19 resides.

Figure 4-1   Location of Host 128.200.100.100/19

The following list describes the process demonstrated in the video:

1. Write down the mask and IP address in a table, in dotted-decimal format.

2. Find the interesting octet of the mask—the octet that is neither 255 nor 0—and draw a rectangle around that column of the table.

3. Write down values for three octets of the subnet number, as follows:

    a) For octets to the left of the rectangle, copy the IP address's value.

    b) For octets to the right of the rectangle, write down 0s.

4. For the interesting octet's value:

    a) Calculate the magic number (256 minus the mask's value in the interesting octet).

    b) Calculate the integer multiples of the magic number, starting at 0, through 256.

    c) Find the multiple that is closest to the IP address's value in the interesting octet, but not bigger than the IP address's value. Write this multiple down as the subnet number's value in the interesting octet.

Figure 4-2 shows work in progress with the process shown in this video, after the completion of Step 3.

Figure 4-2   Work in Progress Through Step 3

Figure 4-3 shows some of the final work to finish the process and identify the resident subnet.

Figure 4-3   Work in Progress, Through Completion

Finding the Broadcast Address and Range of Addresses in a Subnet

This *CCNA Video Mentor* (CVM) lab explains how to find a subnet's broadcast address, which then enables you to find the range of addresses in the subnet that can be assigned to hosts in that subnet. In particular, it shows you how to find the broadcast address and range of addresses for subnet 128.200.96.0, mask 255.255.224.0.

Note that Lab 4, "Finding the Subnet Number," shows you how to find this particular subnet number, given an IP address in the subnet—address 128.200.100.100 is used in Lab 4. You should watch Lab 4 before watching this video.

The objectives of this lab are as follows:

- To help you understand how to use a particular process (found in the Cisco Press *CCENT/CCNA ICND1 Official Exam Certification Guide*) to find a subnet's broadcast address and the range of usable addresses in the subnet

- To help you understand how to find the answers to this kind of question quickly, accurately, and with confidence

Scenario

This lab contains a single step, focusing on the process by which to find the broadcast address (128.200.127.255) of a given subnet (128.200.96.0/19).

Video Presentation Reference

The video presents figures, tables, and text with short lectures before showing the CLI of the router. This section simply lists these figures and tables for reference.

Figure 5-1 shows a figure used in the video to demonstrate the original purpose of the subnet broadcast address.

Figure 5-1   Flow of a Packet Sent to a Subnet Broadcast Address

Subnet 128.200.96.0/19
Subnet Broadcast Address: 128.200.127.255

This video demonstrates Steps 5, 6, and 7 from the following process. Steps 1 through 4 were demonstrated in Lab 4 and are listed here for convenient reference:

1. Write down the mask and IP address in a table, in dotted-decimal format.

2. Find the interesting octet of the mask—the octet that is neither 255 nor 0—and draw a rectangle around that column of the table.

3. Write down values for three octets of the subnet number, as follows:

   a) For octets to the left of the rectangle, copy the IP address's value.

   b) For octets to the right of the rectangle, write down 0s.

4. For the interesting octet's value:

   a) Calculate the magic number (256 minus the mask's value in the interesting octet).

   b) Calculate the integer multiples of the magic number, starting at 0, through 256.

   c) Find the multiple that is closest to the IP address's value in the interesting octet, but not bigger than the IP address's value. Write this multiple down as the subnet number's value in the interesting octet.

5. To find the subnet broadcast address:

   a) For octets to the left of the rectangle, copy the subnet number or IP address's value.

   b) For octets to the right of the rectangle, write down 255s.

   c) In the interesting octet, add the subnet number's value to the magic number and subtract 1.

6. For the first IP address in the range of addresses, copy the subnet number but add 1 to the fourth octet.

7. For the last IP address in the range of addresses, copy the subnet broadcast address but subtract 1 from the fourth octet.

Figure 5-2 shows work in progress after Steps 5A and 5B.

Figure 5-2   **Work in Progress Through Step 5B**

Mask: 255.255.224.0
IP Address: 128.200.100.100

Interesting Octet

Subnet Mask	255	255	224	0
IP Address	128	200	100	100
Subnet Number	128	200	96	0
First IP Address				
Last IP Address				
Broadcast Address	128	200		255

5b) For mask octets to the right of the rectangle, write down 255.

5a) For mask octets to the left of the rectangle, copy subnet number's octets.

Figure 5-3 shows some of the work required at Step 5C, the trickiest part of the process.

Figure 5-3   **Work in Progress, Step 5C**

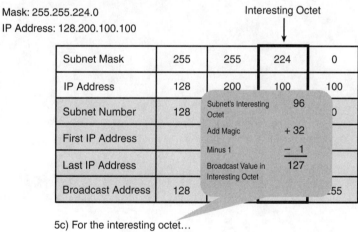

Mask: 255.255.224.0
IP Address: 128.200.100.100

Interesting Octet

Subnet Mask	255	255	224	0
IP Address	128	200	100	100
Subnet Number	128		96	0
First IP Address				
Last IP Address				
Broadcast Address	128			255

Subnet's Interesting Octet   96
Add Magic   + 32
Minus 1   − 1
Broadcast Value in Interesting Octet   127

5c) For the interesting octet…

Magic = 256 − 224 = 32

Lab 6

Finding All Subnets of a Network with Less Than 8 Subnet Bits

This *CCNA Video Mentor* (CVM) lab explains how to find all subnets of a single classful IP network, assuming that a single mask is used throughout the network and that the mask implies fewer than eight subnet bits. The process shown in this lab, like Labs 4 and 5, is the same process described in the Cisco Press *CCENT/CCNA ICND1 Official Exam Certification Guide*. As such, it is best to view this video after viewing Labs 4 and 5.

This video shows you how to find all subnets of Class B network 128.200.0.0, with mask 255.255.224.0.

The objectives of this lab are as follows:

- To help you understand how to use a particular process (found in the Cisco Press *CCENT/CCNA ICND1 Official Exam Certification Guide*) to find all subnets of a single IP network

- To show how to identify the zero and broadcast subnets

- To help you understand how to find the answers to this kind of question quickly and with confidence

Scenario

This lab contains a single step that shows how to find all the subnets of a single classful network.

Video Presentation Reference

The video presents figures, tables, and text with short lectures before showing the CLI of the router. This section simply lists these figures and tables for reference.

The process demonstrated in this video is summarized in the following list:

1. Write down the mask in a table, in dotted-decimal format.

2. Find the interesting octet of the mask—the octet that is neither 255 nor 0—and draw a rectangle around that column of the table.

3. Calculate the magic number (256 minus the mask's value in the interesting octet).

4. Write down the classful network number in the row labeled Zero Subnet.

5. To find each successive subnet number:

   a) Copy the previous subnet number's three boring octets.

   b) For the interesting octet, add the magic number to the previous subnet's interesting octet value.

6. When Step 5b's sum is 256, stop. The subnet found before the sum of 256 is the last subnet, namely the broadcast subnet.

Figure 6-1 shows work in progress through Step 4.

Figure 6-1   Work in Progress Through Step 4

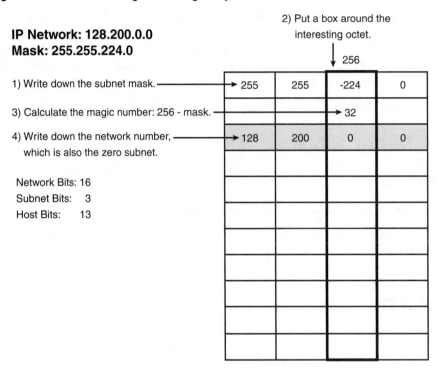

Figure 6-2 shows work in progress after the first pass through Step 5.

Figure 6-2   **Work in Progress After First Pass Through Step 5**

	255	255	224	0
Mask	255	255	224	0
Magic Number			32	
Network Number/Zero Subnet	128	200	+0	0
5a) Copy previous subnet's three uninteresting octets. →128	128	200	32	0
5b) Add the magic number to the previous subnet's interesting octet.				

Figure 6-3 shows work in progress after the second pass through Step 5.

Figure 6-3   **Work in Progress After Second Pass Through Step 5**

	255	255	224	0
Mask	255	255	224	0
Magic Number			32	
Network Number/Zero Subnet	128	200	0	0
	128	200	32	0
5a) Copy the previous subnet's three uninteresting octets. → 128	128	200	+32 64	0
5b) Add the magic number to the previous subnet's interesting octet.				

Figure 6-4 shows work in progress after Step 6, which tells you when to stop the process.

Figure 6-4   Work in Progress After Step 6

Mask	255	255	224	0

Magic Number			32	

Network Number/Zero Subnet	128	200	0	0
	128	200	32	0
	128	200	64	0
	128	200	96	0
	128	200	128	0
	128	200	160	0
	128	200	192	0
Broadcast Subnet	128	200	224	0

6) 256 is out of range – this is not a valid subnet number.

Figure 6-5 shows the list of eight subnets, as well as the zero subnet and broadcast subnet.

Figure 6-5   Answer: A List of Subnets

Zero Subnet	128	200	0	0
	128	200	32	0
	128	200	64	0
	128	200	96	0
	128	200	128	0
	128	200	160	0
	128	200	192	0
Broadcast Subnet	128	200	224	0

IP Subnet Design and Implementation

This *CCNA Video Mentor* (CVM) lab explains how to find all subnets of a single classful IP network, assuming that a single mask is used throughout the network and that the mask implies fewer than eight subnet bits. The process shown in this lab, like Labs 4 and 5, is the same process described in the Cisco Press *CCENT/CCNA ICND1 Official Exam Certification Guide*. As such, it is best to view this video after viewing Labs 4 and 5.

This video shows you how to find all subnets of class B network 128.200.0.0, with mask 255.255.224.0.

The objectives of this lab are as follows:

- Identify the location of the subnets required for a given network topology.

- Be more familiar with the process of finding all subnets of a network, using a static-length subnet mask.

- Review the process of finding the range of IP addresses in each subnet.

Scenario

This lab contains three steps, as follows:

1. Examine an internetwork design, identifying the number of required subnets and the location of each subnet.

2. Calculate the possible subnet numbers and choose the (numerically) smallest subnets.

3. Assign IP addresses to each router, switch, and host.

Video Presentation Reference

The video presents figures and animation with short lectures. This section simply lists these figures and other information for reference.

Step 1 Reference

Figure 7-1   Topology Reference

Figure 7-2   Location of the Required Subnets

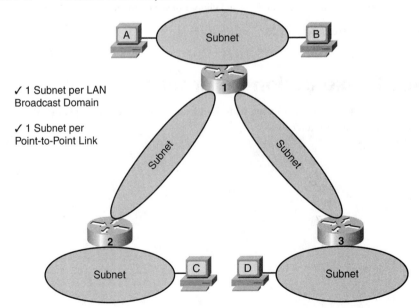

Figure 7-3   **Additional Subnets when Using VLANs**

Step 2 Reference

This step shows another example of the process shown in Lab 6, which explains how to find all subnets of a classful network. The generic process used to find these subnets, which is also found in Lab 6, is as follows:

1. Write down the mask in a table, in dotted-decimal format.

2. Find the interesting octet of the mask—the octet that is neither 255 nor 0—and draw a rectangle around that column of the table.

3. Calculate the magic number (256 minus the mask's value in the interesting octet).

4. Write down the classful network number in the row labeled Zero Subnet.

5. To find each successive subnet number:

   a) Copy the previous subnet number's three boring octets.

   b) For the interesting octet, add the magic number to the previous subnet's interesting octet value.

6. When Step 5b's sum is 256, stop. The subnet found before the sum of 256 is the last subnet, namely the broadcast subnet.

Figure 7-4 shows work in progress through Step 4.

Figure 7-4   Work in Progress Through Step 4

IP Network: 172.20.0.0
Mask: 255.255.255.0

2) Put a box around
the interesting octet.

↓ 256

1) Write down the subnet mask. ────────→ 255 | 255 | -255 | 0

3) Calculate the magic number: 256 - mask. ────────→ 1

4) Write down the network number, ────────→ 172 | 20 | 0 | 0
   which is also the zero subnet.

Use Smallest Numeric
Subnet Numbers

Network Bits: 16
Subnet Bits: 8
Host Bits: 8

Figure 7-5 shows work in progress after completing all passes and finding all subnet numbers.

Figure 7-5   List of All Subnets

	255	255	255	0
Mask	255	255	255	0
Magic Number			1	
Network Number/Zero Subnet	172	20	+0	0
5a) Copy the previous subnet's three uninteresting octets.			1	
	172	20	2	0
	172	20	3	0
	172	20	4	0
	172	20	5	0
5b) Add the magic number to the previous subnet's interesting octet.	172	20	6	0
			...	
	172	20	255	0

Figure 7-6 shows the subnets chosen from the list of subnets and the locations for each subnet.

Figure 7-6   Subnets and Locations in This Video

Step 3 Reference

Table 7-1 lists the six numerically smallest subnet numbers for this video, along with the range of IP addresses and subnet broadcast address for each subnet.

Table 7-1   Numerically Smallest Subnet Numbers, IP Address Range, and Broadcast Address

Subnet Number	Smallest Usable Address	Largest Usable Address	Broadcast Address
172.20.0.0	172.20.0.1	172.20.0.254	172.20.0.255
172.20.1.0	172.20.1.1	172.20.1.254	172.20.1.255
172.20.2.0	172.20.2.1	172.20.2.254	172.20.2.255
172.20.3.0	172.20.3.1	172.20.3.254	172.20.3.255
172.20.4.0	172.20.4.1	172.20.4.254	172.20.4.255
172.20.5.0	172.20.5.1	172.20.5.254	172.20.5.255

Figure 7-7 shows the individual IP addresses chosen to meet the requirements of the network manager—highest IP addresses for the routers, next highest for the switches, and smallest for the hosts.

Figure 7-7   Figure with Actual IP Addresses Listed

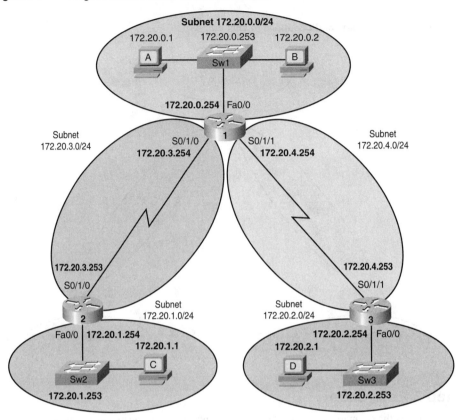

Static and Connected Routes

This *CCNA Video Mentor* (CVM) lab shows how to configure static routes in a simple internetwork. In particular, the objectives of this lab are the following:

- Explain the concept of connected routes

- List the requirements for a router to create a connected route

- Configure an **ip route** command using two different styles:

  - Using a next-hop IP address

  - Using an outgoing interface

- Describe the parts of an individual route

Scenario

This lab contains three main steps, as follows:

Step 1. Show how two routers, when configured with IP addresses on working interfaces, add connected routes to their routing tables.

Step 2. Explain the need for a static route on router R1 to forward packets from left-to-right in the network used in this lab and see how to configure and verify that static route.

Step 3. Explain the need for a static route on router R2 to forward packets from right-to-left in the network used in this lab. Then see how to configure and verify that static route, this time using the outgoing interface option in the **ip route** command.

Initial Configurations

Examples 8-1 and 8-2 show the pertinent configurations of routers R1 and R2 for this lab. As usual, the parts of the configurations not relevant to this lab have been omitted.

```
Example 8-1    Initial Configuration for R1

hostname R1
!
interface FastEthernet 0/0
 ip address 172.22.11.1 255.255.255.0
!
interface Serial 0/1/0
 ip address 172.22.112.1 255.255.255.0
```

Example 8-1   Initial Configuration for R1 *continued*

```
!
interface Serial 0/1/1
  ip address 172.22.113.1 255.255.255.0
  shutdown
```

Example 8-2   Initial Configuration for R2

```
hostname R2
!
interface FastEthernet 0/0
  ip address 172.22.12.2 255.255.255.0
!
interface Serial 0/1/0
  ip address 172.22.112.2 255.255.255.0
```

Ending Configurations

None of the initial configuration is changed. However, Examples 8-3 and 8-4 show the configuration added to R1 and R2, respectively, by the end of the lab video.

Example 8-3   Configuration Added to R1 During the Lab Video

```
ip route 172.22.12.0 255.255.255.0 172.22.112.2
```

Example 8-4   Configuration Added to R2 During the Lab Video

```
ip route 172.22.11.0 255.255.255.0 S0/1/0
```

Video Presentation Reference

This video presents several figures that describe the internetwork and the need for additional routes on the routers. This section simply lists these figures for reference.

Figure 8-1 shows a diagram of the network used in this example.

Figure 8-1   Lab 5 Network Topology

All Interfaces/Subnets Use a /24 (255.255.255.0) Mask

Because the video is organized into three separate steps, the reference materials have been organized into three separate sections.

Step 1 Reference

Figure 8-2   Analysis of Connected Routes

All Interfaces/Subnets Use a /24 (255.255.255.0) Mask

Subnet 172.22.11.0/24   Subnet 172.22.112.0/24   Subnet 172.22.12.0/24

R1 Routing Table

Subnet	Next-Hop	Int.
172.22.11.0/24	(Connected)	Fa0/0
172.22.112.0/24	(Connected)	S0/1/0

R2 Routing Table

Subnet	Next-Hop	Int.
172.22.112.0/24	(Connected)	S0/1/0
172.22.12.0/24	(Connected)	Fa0/0

Requirements to Add a Connected Route:
1) IP address is configured on the interface.
2) Interface is "UP and UP."

Step 2 Reference

Figure 8-3   Need for a Static Route to 172.22.12.0/24

Figure 8-4   ip route Command with Next-hop

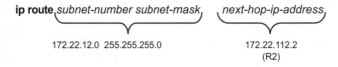

Step 3 Reference

Figure 8-5   Need for a Static Route to 172.22.11.0/24

Figure 8-6   ip route Command with Outgoing Interface

RIP Configuration

This *CCNA Video Mentor* lab shows how to configure RIP Version 1 (V1) in an internetwork that uses two alternative IP addressing schemes. The objectives of this lab are as follows:

- Configure the RIP **network** command.
- Describe how a router interprets the RIP **network** command.
- Describe some of the key information in the output of the **show ip protocols** command.
- Compare the default RIP version behavior to a router that has been configured to use only RIP version 2.

Scenario

This lab contains two main steps, as follows:

Step 1. Configure RIP in a network that uses only subnets of Class B network 172.22.0.0, with default version settings.

Step 2. See the effects of mismatched versions, and migrate to Version 2.

Initial Configurations

Examples 9-1 through 9-3 show the pertinent initial configurations of Routers R1, R2, and R3 in the lab video. Note that this lab begins with these three routers having the correct IP addresses configured, along with the initial RIP configuration on Router R3, to match the topology illustrated later in the chapter in Figure 9-1. As usual, the parts of the configurations not relevant to this lab have been omitted.

Example 9-1   Initial Configuration for R1

```
hostname R1
!
interface FastEthernet 0/0
 ip address 172.22.11.1 255.255.255.0
!
interface serial 0/1/0
 ip address 172.22.112.1 255.255.255.0
 clock rate 1536000
!
interface serial 0/1/1
 ip address 172.22.113.1 255.255.255.0
 clock rate 1536000
```

Example 9-2   Initial Configuration for R2

```
hostname R2
!
interface FastEthernet 0/0
 ip address 172.22.12.2 255.255.255.0
!
interface serial 0/1/0
 ip address 172.22.112.2 255.255.255.0
!
interface serial 0/1/1
 ip address 172.22.123.2 255.255.255.0
 clock rate 1536000
```

Example 9-3   Initial Configuration for R3

```
hostname R3
!
interface FastEthernet 0/0
 ip address 172.22.13.3 255.255.255.0
!
interface serial 0/1/0
 ip address 172.22.123.3 255.255.255.0
!
interface serial 0/1/1
 ip address 172.22.113.3 255.255.255.0
!
router rip
 version 2
 network 172.22.0.0
```

Configuration After Lab Step 1

This lab adds configuration at both Step 1 and Step 2. Example 9-4 shows the configuration added to R1 during Step 1. Example 9-5 shows the configuration added to R2 at Step 1.

Example 9-4   Configuration Added to R1 During Step 1

```
router rip
 network 172.22.0.0
```

Example 9-5   Configuration Added to R2 During Step 1

```
router rip
 network 172.22.0.0
```

Ending Configurations

This lab adds the RIP **version 2** command to both R1's and R2's RIP configuration as part of Step 2. Example 9-6, 9-7, and 9-8 list the ending RIP configuration on Routers R1, R2, and R3, for easy reference.

Example 9-6   Ending RIP Configuration on R1

```
router rip
 version 2
 network 192.22.0.0
```

Example 9-7   Ending Configuration on R2

```
router rip
 version 2
 network 192.22.0.0
```

Example 9-8   Ending Configuration on R3

```
router rip
 version 2
 network 192.22.0.0
```

Video Presentation Reference

This video includes several figures that contain the same images used in the lab video. Because the video is organized into two separate steps, the reference materials have been organized into two separate sections. Each section simply lists these figures and tables for reference.

Step 1 Reference

Figure 9-1   Three Routers, Six Subnets of Class B Network 172.22.0.0

Figure 9-2   Subnet Reference for Step 1

Figure 9-3   Format of the RIP network Command

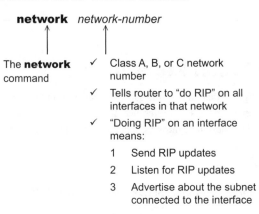

Figure 9-4   **Impact of the RIP network Command: R1, Step 1**

Step 2 Reference

Figure 9-5   **Effect of Version 2 Updates Sent to R1 and R2**

Figure 9-6   Effect of Version 1 Updates Sent to R3

Default Settings:
 • Send V1
 • Receive Either V1 or V2

V1

V1   V1

router rip
network 172.22.0.0

V1 update received
– IGNORE!

With **version 2**
Command Configured:
 • Send V2 Only
 • Receive V2 Only

router rip
version 2
network 172.22.0.0

The CCNA certification can be achieved through two different paths: by taking the single CCNA (640-802) exam or by taking both the ICND1 (640-822) and ICND2 (640-816) exams. This product separates the video labs into two sections, with labs focusing on the ICND2 exam in this section and labs focusing on the ICND1 exam in the other section. The labs in both sections apply to the CCNA exam.

Part I   LANs

Lab 1   Configuring VLANs

Lab 2   VTP Servers and Clients

Part II   Routing and Routing Protocols

Lab 3   RIP with Split Horizon, Route Poisoning, and Poison Reverse

Lab 4   Single Area and Multi-area OSPF Configuration

Lab 5   EIGRP Configuration and Operation

Lab 6   Understanding EIGRP Metric Calculations

Part III   Scaling IP Addresses

Lab 7   NAT Overload (PAT)

Lab 8   IPv6 Subnetting and Address Configuration

Part IV   WAN

Lab 9   PPP and CHAP Configuration

Part V   Security

Lab 10 Access Lists

Lab 11 Access Lists II

Configuring VLANs

This *CCNA Video Mentor* lab shows how to use the commands required to configure virtual LANs (VLANs) on Cisco IOS Software-based switches, in addition to a few of the commands used to examine VLAN operations. In particular, the objectives of this lab are as follows:

- Configure VLANs on Cisco switches

- Configure the VTP mode on Cisco switches

- Determine the status of VLAN trunks

- Configure 802.1Q trunking between two Cisco switches

Scenario

This lab contains two main steps, as follows:

Step 1. Use a *three-step process* to create the first VLAN on a switch:

Configure VTP mode

Create a VLAN

Add interfaces to that VLAN

Step 2. Examine and configure *802.1Q trunking* between two switches

Initial Configurations

The two switches in this lab begin with some basic configuration. First, host switches have their hostnames configured. Second, the switch ports connected to the PCs have been configured to use the **spanning-tree portfast** command, which causes these end-user ports not to wait on Spanning Tree Protocol (STP) timers when the ports are administratively enabled. However, all VLAN configurations has been removed before this lab begins. Examples 1-1 and 1-2 show the basic initial configurations for both switches in this lab.

Example 1-1   Initial Configuration for Sw1

```
hostname Sw1
!
interface FastEthernet 0/11
 spanning-tree portfast
!
interface FastEthernet 0/13
```

Example 1-1   Initial Configuration for Sw1   *continued*

```
 spanning-tree portfast
!
interface vlan 1
 ip address 172.30.1.101 255.255.255.0
 no shutdown
!
ip default-gateway 172.30.1.251
```

Example 1-2   Initial Configuration for Sw2

```
hostname Sw2
!
interface FastEthernet 0/12
 spanning-tree portfast
!
interface vlan 1
 ip address 172.30.1.102 255.255.255.0
 no shutdown
!
ip default-gateway 172.30.1.251
```

Ending Configurations

This lab adds some configuration commands to both Sw1 and Sw2; however, it does not change any of the earlier configurations. Examples 1-3 and 1-4 show the configuration added during the lab.

Example 1-3   Configuration on Sw1 Added During this Lab

```
vtp transparent
!
vlan 11
 name thisisvlan11
!
interface FastEthernet 0/11
 switchport access vlan 11
!
interface FastEthernet 0/13
 switchport access vlan 11
!
interface FastEthernet 0/23
 switchport mode trunk
```

Example 1-4   Configuration on Sw2 Added During this Lab

```
vtp transparent
!
vlan 11
!
interface FastEthernet 0/12
 switchport access vlan 11
```

Video Presentation Reference

This video presents several figures and a table that support the concepts covered in the lab. This section simply lists these figures for reference. Because the video is organized into three separate steps, the reference materials have been organized into three separate sections.

Step 1 Reference

Figure 1-1   Step 1 Topology and Configuration Steps

PC1
0011.1111.1111
172.30.1.1

Fa0/11

PC3   Fa0/13
0033.3333.3333
172.30.1.3   Sw1
Fa0/23

trunk

Fa0/24

Sw2
Fa0/12

0022.2222.222
172.30.1.2

PC2

Sw1 Configuration:
1 Enable VTP transparent mode
2 Create VLAN 11
3 Put Fa0/11 and Fa0/13 into VLAN 11
**Repeat 2 and 3 for
each new VLAN**

Trunk Configuration:
➢ Defaults to "Dynamic desirable"
    — trunks automatically

Sw2 Configuration:
1 Enable VTP transparent mode
2 Automatically create VLAN 11 by putting
    interface Fa0/12 into VLAN 11

Step 2 Reference

Table 1-1   The Meaning of the *type* Option of the switchport mode Command

Value of the *type* Keyword	Meaning of the *type* Keyword
access	Always do *not* trunk
trunk	Always trunk
dynamic desirable	Negotiate whether to trunk or not and initiate the process
dynamic auto	Negotiate whether to trunk or not but do not initiate the process

Table 1-2   Trunk Configuration Options for Making Two LAN Switches Trunk

SW1 Configuration for Trunking Mode	Required Setting on SW2 to Trunk
access	None—cannot trunk
trunk	Trunk, dynamic desirable, or dynamic auto
dynamic desirable	Trunk, dynamic desirable, or dynamic auto
dynamic auto	Trunk or dynamic desirable

VTP Servers and Clients

This *CCNA Video Mentor* lab explains how to configure VTP servers and clients, lists the requirements that must be met for those switches to exchange VLAN information, and explains how to use **show** commands to confirm that the switches have learned about new VLANs. In particular, the objectives of this lab are as follows:

- Configure VTP on Cisco switches.

- Verify whether the switches meet the required conditions that enable VTP to work between two switches.

- Verify that a VTP client has learned VLAN information from a VTP peer.

Scenario

This lab contains three main steps, as follows:

Step 1.   Configure one switch as a VTP server and another as a VTP client.

Step 2.   Complete all VTP requirements by configuring trunking between two switches.

Step 3.   Configure VLANs on the VTP server and confirm that the VTP client has learned about the VLANs.

Initial Configurations

The two 2960 switches in this lab begin with some basic configuration, but with all default settings related to VTP and the VLAN database. Both switches have their hostnames configured, and each has an IP address assigned to its respective VLAN 1 interface. Example 2-1 and Example 2-2 show the basic initial configurations for both switches in this lab.

Example 2-1   Initial Configuration for Sw1

```
hostname Sw1
!
interface vlan 1
 ip address 172.30.1.101 255.255.255.0
 no shutdown
```

Example 2-2   Initial Configuration for Sw2

```
hostname Sw2
!
interface vlan 1
 ip address 172.30.1.102 255.255.255.0
 no shutdown
```

Ending Configurations

This lab adds some configuration commands to both Sw1 and Sw2; however, it does not change any of the earlier configurations. Example 2-3 and Example 2-4 show the configuration added during the lab.

Example 2-3   Configuration on Sw1 Added During This Lab

```
vtp domain Fred
vtp password Barney
!
vlan 2
 name Wilma
!
interface gigabitEthernet 0/1
 switchport mode trunk
!
interface fastethernet 0/1
 switchport access vlan 2
```

Example 2-4 shows the ending configuration on Sw2; however, note that the video shows the configuration of the **vtp domain fred** command, which is later replaced with the **vtp domain Fred** command.

Example 2-4   Configuration on Sw2 Added During This Lab

```
vtp mode client
vtp domain Fred
vtp password Barney
!
interface fastethernet 0/2
 switchport access vlan 2
```

Video Presentation Reference

This video presents several figures and a table that support the concepts covered in the lab. This section simply lists these figures for reference. Because the video is organized into three separate steps, the reference materials have been organized into three separate sections.

Step 1 Reference

Figure 2-1   Step 1 Topology and Configuration

Sw1 VTP Server Configuration:
1) Defaults to VTP server mode
2) Assign domain name "Fred"
3) Assign password "Barney"

IP Adresses

Sw2 VTP Client Configuration:
1) Enable VTP client mode
2) Assign domain name "fred"
3) Assign password "Barney"

Step 2 Reference

Figure 2-2   Requirements for VTP to Work Properly

Send VTP messages on trunks, and only trunks!

VTP Requirements
1) Same domain name
2) Same password (if used on either switch)
3) Messages sent only over operational trunks

Step 3 Reference

Figure 2-3   VLAN Configuration Process Shown in This Video

Assign to VLAN 2 with **switchport access vlan 2** command.

Add VLAN 2 with the **vlan 2** command.

VTP Revision Number: 0 + 1 = 1

VTP Messages with New VLAN Database

VTP Revision Number = 1
New VLAN 2 Learned

Assign to VLAN 2 with **switchport access vlan 2** command.

RIP V1 with Split Horizon, Route Poisoning, and Poison Reverse

This *CCNA Video Mentor* lab helps you build a deeper understanding of RIP operations, particularly of the effect of distance vector loop-avoidance mechanisms. The lab begins with a small working internetwork using RIP. Then the lab explains how RIP works when all links are up and working and how RIP works when a link fails. In particular, this lab covers the following:

- Interpret the contents of the routing table using the **show ip route** command

- Determine which RIP update sources continue to send periodic updates using the **show ip protocols** command

- Interpret debug messages that show the effects of

  — Split horizon

  — Route poisoning

  — Poison reverse

  — Triggered updates

Scenario

This lab contains three main steps, as follows:

Step 1. A description of an internetwork topology—including descriptions of the routes learned by each router—and ways to confirm that RIP continues to send periodic routing updates.

Step 2. A description of split horizon, with router **debug** messages showing the effects of split horizon on the internetwork

Step 3. A description of triggered updates, poison routes, and poison reverse routes, followed by router **debug** command output that shows all of these features.

Initial Configurations

Example 3-1 shows the initial configuration of router R2 at the beginning of the lab. Note that only the pertinent configuration is shown. Similarly, Example 3-2 shows the initial configuration of R3. As usual, the parts of the configurations that are not relevant to this lab have been omitted.

Example 3-1   Initial Configuration for R2

```
interface fastethernet0/0
 ip address 192.168.2.2 255.255.255.0
!
interface serial 0/1/1
 ip address 192.168.4.9 255.255.255.252
 clock rate 1536000
!
interface serial 0/1/0
 description link connected to router R1 - not used in this lab
 shutdown
!
router rip
 network 192.168.2.0
 network 192.168.4.0
```

Example 3-2   Initial Configuration for R3

```
interface fastethernet0/0
 ip address 192.168.3.3 255.255.255.0
!
interface fastethernet0/1
 ip address 192.168.33.3 255.255.255.0
!
interface serial 0/1/0
 ip address 192.168.4.10 255.255.255.252
!
interface serial 0/1/1
! description link connected to router R1 - not used in this lab
 shutdown
!
router rip
 network 192.168.3.0
 network 192.168.33.0
 network 192.168.4.0
```

Ending Configurations

This lab does not change the routers' configurations, other than to shut down the fa0/1 interface on R3 to demonstrate what happens with RIP.

Video Presentation Reference

This video presents several figures that describe the internetwork and the need for additional routes on the routers. This section simply lists these figures for reference.

Because the video is organized into three separate steps, the reference materials have been organized into three separate sections.

Step 1 Reference

Figure 3-1   Lab 7 Topology

Step 2 Reference

Figure 3-2   Split Horizon on R2

R2 Routing Table

Subnet	Next-Hop	Out. Int.	Metric
192.168.2.0/24	(Connected)	Fa0/0	N/A
192.168.33.0/24	192.168.4.10	S0/1/1	1
192.168.3.0/24	192.168.4.10	S0/1/1	1
192.168.4.8/30	(Connected)	S0/1/1	N/A

Split Horizon:

For an update sent out **S0/1/1,** do not advertise routes whose outgoing interface is **S0/1/1**

RIP V1 Update – Sent out S0/1/1

Subnet	Metric
192.168.2.0	1

Figure 3-3   Split Horizon on R3

Split Horizon:

For an update sent out **S0/1/0,** do not advertise routes whose outgoing interface is **S0/1/0**

R3 Routing Table

Subnet	Next-Hop	Out. Int.	Metric
192.168.3.0/24	(Connected)	Fa0/0	N/A
192.168.33.0/24	(Connected)	Fa0/1	N/A
192.168.2.0/24	192.168.4.9	S0/1/0	1
192.168.4.8/30	(Connected)	S0/1/0	N/A

RIP V1 Update – Sent out S0/1/0

Subnet	Metric
192.168.3.0	1
192.168.33.0	1

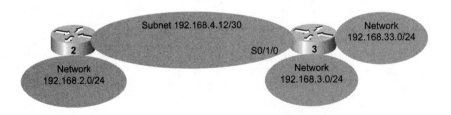

Step 3 Reference

Figure 3-4   Triggered Updates and Route Poisoning

<u>Storyline:</u>

Ⓐ R3's Fa0/0 fails.

Ⓑ R3 sends triggered update (contains only a poisoned route).

Ⓒ R2 sends triggered update. (R2 suspends Split Horizon rules, and poisons route—called a poison reverse route.)

Figure 3-5   Split Horizon with Poison Reverse

Normal Periodic Update – does not list 192.168.3.0

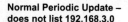

Subnet	Metric
192.168.2.0	1

Triggered Update, Poison Reverse

Subnet	Metric
192.168.3.0	16

Ongoing Periodic Updates

Subnet	Metric
192.168.2.0	1
192.168.3.0	16

Single Area and Multi-area OSPF Configuration

This *CCNA Video Mentor* lab shows how to configure OSPF using several different styles of OSPF **network** commands, both for a single area and for multiple areas. In particular, the objectives of this lab are the following:

- Configure the OSPF **network** command to correctly match an interface and place it into the correct area

- Describe generally how the wildcard mask controls how the OSPF **network** command works

- Configure an Area Border Router (ABR) by placing different interfaces in different areas

- Distinguish between intra-area and interarea OSPF-learned routes

- Describe how a router picks its router ID (RID)

Scenario

This lab contains three main steps, as follows:

Step 1.   Examine the single-area OSPF configuration on three routers (R1, R2, and R3)

Step 2.   Configure an Area Border Router (ABR) to be connected to multiple OSPF areas

Step 3.   Analyze how a router chooses its OSPF RID and verify the RID chosen by a router

Initial Configurations: Lab Step 1

Examples 4-1 through 4-3 show the pertinent initial configurations of routers R1, R2, and R3. All routers begin with all pertinent IP addresses configured, all necessary links up, and OSPF configured to put all links into area 0, as illustrated in Figure 4-1. As usual, the parts of the configurations not relevant to this lab have been omitted.

Example 4-1   Initial Configuration for R1

```
hostname R1
!
interface FastEthernet 0/0
 ip address 172.22.11.1 255.255.255.0
!
interface FastEthernet 0/1
 ip address 172.22.10.1 255.255.255.0
!
interface loopback 1
 ip address 11.11.11.11 255.255.255.0
!
interface loopback 2
 ip address 1.1.1.1 255.255.255.0
!
router ospf 1
 network 172.22.11.1 0.0.0.0 area 0
 network 172.22.10.1 0.0.0.0 area 0
```

Example 4-2   Initial Configuration for R2

```
interface FastEthernet 0/0
 ip address 172.22.12.2 255.255.255.0
!
interface FastEthernet 0/1
 ip address 172.22.10.2 255.255.255.0
!
interface loopback 1
 ip address 2.2.2.2 255.255.255.0
!
router ospf 1
 network 0.0.0.0 255.255.255.255 area 0
```

Example 4-3   Initial Configuration for R3

```
interface FastEthernet 0/0
 ip address 172.22.13.3 255.255.255.0
!
interface FastEthernet 0/1
 ip address 172.22.10.3 255.255.255.0
!
router ospf 2
 network 172.22.0.0  0.0.255.255 area 0
```

Initial Configurations: Lab Step 2

Lab 4's second step adds routers R5 and R6 to the network topology. Examples 4-4 and 4-5 show the initial configurations on these routers needed to begin Step 2. Both routers begin with all pertinent IP addresses configured and all necessary links up, but OSPF is configured on R6 only. The OSPF configuration matches the design shown in Figure 4-1.

Example 4-4   R5 Initial Configuration Needed to Begin Step 2

```
hostname R5
!
interface Serial0/0
 ip address 172.22.115.5 255.255.255.0
!
interface FastEthernet0/0
 ip address 172.22.15.5 255.255.255.0
```

Example 4-6   R6 Initial Configuration Needed to Begin Step 2

```
hostname R6
!
interface Serial0/0
 ip address 172.22.116.6 255.255.255.0
!
interface FastEthernet0/0
 ip address 172.22.16.6 255.255.255.0
!
router ospf 1
 network 0.0.0.0 255.255.255.255 area 6
```

Ending Configurations

This lab video ends with R1 having added configuration to support areas 5 and 6 and with OSPF configuration having been added to router R5. Example 4-6 shows the configuration added to R1, with Example 4-7 showing all pertinent configuration of R5.

Example 4-6   Configuration Added to R1 During the Video

```
interface Serial0/1/0
 ip address 172.22.115.1 255.255.255.0
 clock rate 1536000
 no shutdown
!
```

Example 4-6   Configuration Added to R1 During the Video   *continued*

```
interface Serial0/1/1
 ip address 172.22.116.1 255.255.255.0
 clock rate 1536000
 no shutdown
!
router ospf 1
 network 172.22.115.1 0.0.0.0 area 5
 network 172.22.116.1 0.0.0.0 area 6
```

Example 4-7   Configuration Added to R5 During the Video

```
router ospf 1
 network 0.0.0.0 255.255.255.255 area 5
```

Video Presentation Reference

This video includes several figures and one table that both help explain the scenario in the lab and list important reference information.

Because the video is organized into three separate steps, the reference materials have been organized into three separate sections. Each section simply lists these figures and tables for reference.

Step 1 Reference

Figure 4-1   Three Routers and Four LAN Subnets Used in Step 1

Figure 4-2   Subnets and OSPF Areas Used in Step 1

All Subnets Use a /24 (255.255.255.0) Subnet Mask

Figure 4-3   Format of the OSPF network Command

Table 4-1   Sample OSPF network Command Wildcard Masks and Their Meanings

Wildcard Mask	Meaning
0.0.0.0	Compare the entire address
0.0.0.255	Compare the first 3 octets only
0.0.255.255	Compare the first 2 octets only
0.255.255.255	Compare the first octet only
255.255.255.255	No need to compare anything—all addresses are considered to match

Step 2 Reference

Figure 4-4   **Expanded Topology for Step 2**

Figure 4-5   **Subnet Numbers in Step 2**

Figure 4-6   Area Design for Expanded Topology

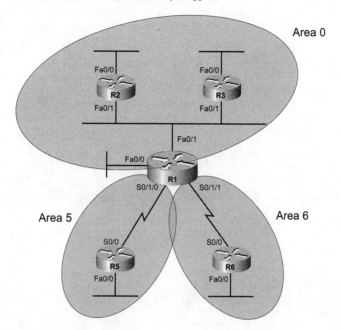

Step 3 Reference

OSPF chooses its router ID using the following sequence of choices:

1. As configured with the OSPF **router-id** command (as configured under the **router ospf** command).

2. If the **router-id** command is not configured, the router uses the highest IP address of all "up/up" loopback interfaces.

3. If steps 1 and 2 do not define the OSPF RID, the router uses the highest IP address of all "up/up" non-loopback interfaces.

Figure 4-7   Examples of OSPF Router ID Choices

Lab 5

EIGRP Configuration and Operation

This *CCNA Video Mentor* lab shows how to configure EIGRP in an internetwork having one Class B network that uses variable-length subnet masks (VLSM). The objectives of this lab are as follows:

- Configure the EIGRP **network** command
- Confirm on which interfaces a router has enabled EIGRP
- Interpret the **show ip route** command output when VLSM are used

Scenario

This lab contains two main steps, as follows:

Step 1. Configure EIGRP in a network that uses only subnets of the Class B network 172.22.0.0

Step 2. Discover the impact when a router does not enable EIGRP on an interface

Initial Configurations

Examples 5-1 through 5-3 show the pertinent initial configurations of routers R1, R2, and R3 in the lab video. Note that this lab begins with these three routers having the correct IP addresses configured, but only router R2 has been configured for EIGRP. As usual, the parts of the configurations not relevant to this lab have been omitted.

Example 5-1   Initial Configuration for R1

```
hostname R1
!
interface FastEthernet 0/0
 ip address 172.22.11.1 255.255.255.128
!
interface serial 0/1/0
 ip address 172.22.112.101 255.255.255.252
 clock rate 1536000
!
interface serial 0/1/1
 ip address 172.22.113.209 255.255.255.252
 clock rate 1536000
```

Example 5-2   Initial Configuration for R2

```
hostname R2
!
interface FastEthernet 0/0
 ip address 172.22.12.202 255.255.255.192
!
interface serial 0/1/0
 ip address 172.22.112.102 255.255.255.252
!
interface serial 0/1/1
 ip address 172.22.123.97 255.255.255.252
!
router eigrp 1
 network 172.22.0.0
```

Example 5-3   Initial Configuration for R3

```
hostname R3
!
interface FastEthernet 0/0
 ip address 172.22.13.103 255.255.255.224
!
interface serial 0/1/0
 ip address 172.22.123.98 255.255.255.252
 clock rate 1536000
!
interface serial 0/1/1
 ip address 172.22.113.210 255.255.255.252
```

Ending Configurations

This lab does not change any of the initial configurations in routers R1, R2, or R3. However, it does add to the configurations of R1 and R3, as shown in Examples 5-4 and 5-5.

Example 5-4   Configuration Added to R1 During the Lab

```
router eigrp 1
 network 172.22.0.0
```

Example 5-5   Configuration Added to R3 During the Lab

```
router eigrp 1
  network 172.22.113.0 0.0.0.255
  network 172.22.123.0 0.0.0.255
  network 172.22.13.0 0.0.0.255
```

Video Presentation Reference

This video includes several figures that contain the same images used in the lab video. Because the video is organized into two separate steps, the reference materials have been organized into two separate sections. Each section simply lists these figures and tables for reference.

Step 1 Reference

Figure 5-1   Three Routers, Six Subnets of Class B Network 172.22.0.0

Table 5-1 lists the subnets shown in Figure 5-1.

Table 5-1   Four Key Internet Layer Protocols

Location	Subnet Number	Range of IP Addresses	Subnet Broadcast Address
R1 LAN	172.22.11.0/25	172.22.11.1–172.22.11.126	172.22.11.127
R2 LAN	172.22.12.192/26	172.22.12.193–172.22.12.254	172.22.12.255
R3 LAN	172.22.13.96/27	172.22.13.97–172.22.13.126	172.22.13.127
R1-R2 Serial	172.22.112.100/30	172.22.112.101–172.22.112.102	172.22.112.103
R1-R3 Serial	172.22.113.208/30	172.22.113.209–172.22.113.210	172.22.113.211
R2-R3 Serial	172.22.123.96/30	172.22.123.97–172.22.123.98	172.22.123.99

Figure 5-2　　**Subnet Reference for Step 1**

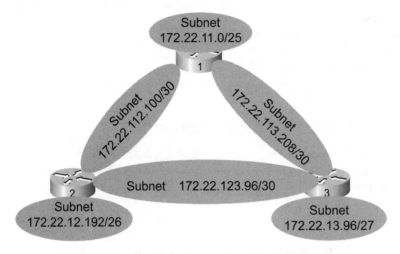

Figure 5-3　　**The Original Format of the EIGRP network Command**

network　　*network-number*

The **network** command

• Class A, B, or C network number

• Tells router to "do EIGRP" on all interfaces in that network

• "Doing EIGRP" on an interface means:
  1. Send EIGRP messages
  2. Listen for EIGRP messages
  3. Advertise about the subnet connected to the interface

Figure 5-4　　**The Newer Format of the EIGRP network Command**

network　　*address*　　*wildcard-mask*

The **network** command

• Any dotted decimal number, typically an IP address or subnet number

• Limits which parts of the network number must match an interface

Figure 5-5   **The Impact of the EIGRP network Command – R1, Step 1**

```
router eigrp 1
  network 172.22.11.0  0.0.0.255
  network 172.22.112.0  0.0.0.255
```

Step 2 Reference

Figure 5-6   **Problem of Not Advertising Subnet 172.22.13.96/27**

Understanding EIGRP Metric Calculations

This *CCNA Video Mentor* lab helps you understand the bandwidth and delay settings on router interfaces and how they impact the metric calculated by the EIGRP routing protocol. In particular, this lab covers the following:

- Determines which interface's bandwidth and delay settings impact EIGRP's metric calculation for a given route.

- Explains how EIGRP uses constraining (slowest) bandwidth but cumulative interface delay.

- Predicts the impact of changing an interface's bandwidth setting on the EIGRP metric calculation.

Scenario

This lab contains two main steps, as follows:

Step 1. Analyze the differences between the EIGRP metrics for two possible routes to reach a single subnet.

Step 2. Predict the change in EIGRP metrics based on a change to an interface's bandwidth setting.

Initial Configurations

Examples 6-1, 6-2, and 6-3 show the pertinent initial configurations of Routers R1, R2, and R3 in the lab video. Note that this lab begins with these three routers having the correct IP addresses configured, and with EIGRP configured and enabled on all interfaces—but with default bandwidth and delay settings. As usual, the parts of the configurations not relevant to this lab have been omitted.

Example 6-1   Initial Configuration for R1

```
hostname R1
!
interface FastEthernet 0/0
 ip address 172.22.11.1 255.255.255.128
!
interface serial 0/1/0
 ip address 172.22.112.101 255.255.255.252
 clock rate 1536000
!
interface serial 0/1/1
 ip address 172.22.113.209 255.255.255.252
 clock rate 1536000
!
router eigrp 1
 network 172.22.0.0
```

Example 6-2   Initial Configuration for R2

```
hostname R2
!
interface FastEthernet 0/0
 ip address 172.22.12.202 255.255.255.192
!
interface serial 0/1/0
 ip address 172.22.112.102 255.255.255.252
!
interface serial 0/1/1
 ip address 172.22.123.97 255.255.255.252
!
router eigrp 1
 network 172.22.0.0
```

Example 6-3   Initial Configuration for R3

```
hostname R3
!
interface FastEthernet 0/0
 ip address 172.22.13.103 255.255.255.224
!
interface serial 0/1/0
 ip address 172.22.123.98 255.255.255.252
 clock rate 1536000
!
interface serial 0/1/1
 ip address 172.22.113.210 255.255.255.252
```

```
!
router eigrp 1
 network 172.22.0.0
```

Ending Configurations

This lab does not change any of the initial configuration, but it does override the default bandwidth setting on R1's S0/1/0 interface. For easy reference, Example 6-4 lists the configuration added during the video.

Example 6-4   Configuration Added to R1 During the Video

```
interface serial 0/1/0
 bandwidth 64
```

Video Presentation Reference

This video presents several figures that describe the internetwork used in the video and how the bandwidth and delay settings impact EIGRP's choice of routes. This section simply lists these figures for reference. Because the video is organized into two separate steps, the reference materials have been organized into two separate sections.

Step 1 Reference

Figure 6-1   Lab 6 Topology and IP Addresses

Figure 6-2   Lab 6 Subnet Number Reference

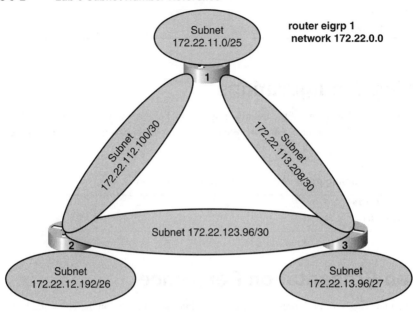

Figure 6-3   Bandwidth Settings That Impact R1's route to Subnet 172.22.12.192/26

Figure 6-4   Bandwidth and Delay Inputs into R1's Two Competing Routes for 172.22.12.192/26

Route to 172.22.12.192/26
Metric Based On:
Slowest Bandwidth: 1544
Cumulative Delay: 2000 + 10 = 2010

Route to 172.22.12.192/26
Metric Based On:
Slowest Bandwidth: 1544
Cumulative Delay: 2000 + 2000 + 10 = 4010

S0/1/0   S0/1/1
bandwidth 1544
delay 2000
bandwidth 1544
delay 2000

delay 2000
bandwidth 11544
S0/1/0

Fa0/0
delay 10
bandwidth 100,000

Figure 6-5   Metric Calculation Reference

$$\text{Metric} = 256 \left(10^7/\text{bandwidth}\right) + 256(\text{delay}) = 2{,}172{,}416$$

Route to 172.22.12.192/26
Metric Based On:
Slowest Bandwidth: 1544
Cumulative Delay: 2000 + 10 = 2010

S0/1/0
bandwidth 1544
delay 2000

bandwidth 1544
S0/1/0

Fa0/0
delay 10
bandwidth 100,000

Step 2 Reference

Figure 6-6   Revised Bandwidth and Delay Inputs

Route to 172.22.12.192/26
Metric Based On:
Slowest Bandwidth: 64
Cumulative Delay: 2000 + 10 = 2010

Route to 172.22.12.192/26
Metric Based On:
Slowest Bandwidth: 1544
Cumulative Delay: 2000 + 2000 + 10 = 4010

S0/1/0
bandwidth 64
delay 2000

S0/1/1
bandwidth 1544
delay 2000

delay 2000
bandwidth 1544
S0/1/0

Fa0/0
delay 10
bandwidth 100,000

NAT Overload (PAT)

This *CCNA Video Mentor* (CVM) lab shows how to configure Network Address Translation (NAT), specifically using the Port Address Translation (PAT) or overload feature. In particular, the objectives of this lab are as follows:

- Define the following NAT terms:

    - Inside, Outside, Inside Local, and Inside Global

- Describe how NAT changes the following:

    - IP addresses for Enterprise (Inside) hosts for a typical Internet connection

    - Port numbers to support thousands of connections using a single Inside Global IP address

- Configure NAT overload (PAT) using a single interface IP address for the Inside Global IP address

Scenario

This lab contains two main steps, as follows:

Step 1. Review the terms associated with the typical use of NAT and PAT with an Internet connection and see NAT working in a router.

Step 2. Review router NAT/PAT configuration using a single IP address on an interface (no NAT pool).

Initial Configurations

Example 7-1 shows the pertinent initial configuration of router R1 in the lab video. Note that this lab begins with R1 having a valid NAT/PAT overload configuration, using the Inside Global IP address of R1's S0/1/0 interface (100.1.1.2). As usual, the parts of the configurations not relevant to this lab have been omitted.

Example 7-1   Initial Configuration for R1

```
hostname R1
!
ip nat inside source list 3 interface serial 0/1/0 overload
!
interface FastEthernet 0/0
 ip address 172.22.11.1 255.255.255.0
 ip nat inside
!
```

Example 7-1   Initial Configuration for R1 *continued*

```
interface Serial 0/1/0
 ip address 100.1.1.2 255.255.255.248
 ip nat outside
!
access-list 3 permit 172.22.0.0 0.0.255.255
```

Ending Configurations

This lab video does not change the router configuration.

Video Presentation Reference

This video presents several figures that describe how NAT overload (PAT) works generally and how it works in the particular example shown in the lab video. This section simply lists these figures for reference.

Figure 7-1 shows a diagram of the network used in this example.

Figure 7-1   Lab 10 Scenario Topology

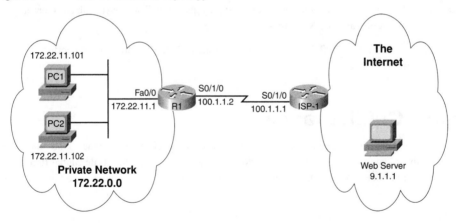

Because the video is organized into two separate steps, the reference materials have been organized into two separate sections.

Step 1 Reference

Figure 7-2   **Concept of Inside and Outside with NAT**

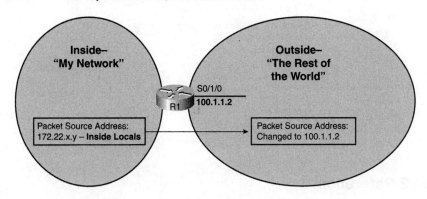

Figure 7-3   **How NAT Overload Changes Inside Addresses and Ports**

Figure 7-4   Three TCP Connections Created to Test NAT Overload

Step 2 Reference

Figure 7-5   Configuring Inside and Outside Interfaces

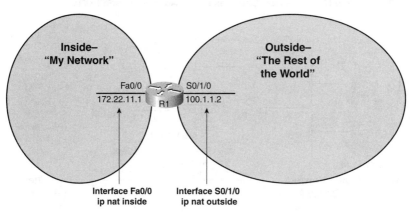

Figure 7-6   Configuring NAT Overload Using an Interface as Inside Global

IPv6 Subnetting and Address Configuration

This *CCNA Video Mentor* lab explains the format of one type of IP Version 6 (IPv6) address, compares the basic concepts of IPv4 and IPv6 subnetting, and shows how to configure IPv6 addresses on Cisco routers. In particular, the objectives of this lab are as follows:

- Describe the general format of IPv6 Global Unicast addresses.
- Describe the similarities between IPv4 and IPv6 subnetting.
- Configure IPv6 addresses on Cisco router interfaces.

Scenario

This lab contains two main steps, as follows:

Step 1.   Compare IPv4 subnetting to IPv6 subnetting in a simple internetwork.

Step 2.   Configure full 128-bit IPv6 addresses on a router.

Initial Configurations

The two routers used in this internetwork begin with IPv4 enabled. Example 8-1 and Example 8-2 list the pertinent IPv4 configuration on these two routers at the beginning of the video.

Example 8-1   Initial (Pertinent) Configuration for R1

```
hostname R1
!
interface Fastethernet 0/0
 ip address 128.107.11.1 255.255.255.0
!
interface Serial 0/1/0
 ip address 128.107.112.1 255.255.255.0
!
router eigrp 1
 network 128.107.0.0
```

Example 8-2   Initial (Pertinent) Configuration for R2

```
hostname R2
!
interface Fastethernet 0/0
```

```
 ip address 128.107.12.2 255.255.255.0
!
interface Serial 0/1/0
 ip address 128.107.112.2 255.255.255.0
!
router eigrp 1
 network 128.107.0.0
```

Ending Configurations

This lab adds a few commands to Router R1 to show the process of enabling IPv6 globally, and one option for how to configure IPv6 interface addresses. Example 8-3 shows the configuration added to R1 during the video.

Example 8-3   Configuration on Sw1 Added During This Lab

```
ipv6 unicast routing
!
interface Fastethernet 0/0
 ipv6 address 2233:0:2222:11::1/64
!
interface Serial 0/1/0
 ipv6 address 2233:0:2222:112::1/64
```

Video Presentation Reference

This video presents several figures that explain concepts and introduce configuration settings. Because the video is organized into two separate steps, the reference materials have been organized into two separate sections.

Step 1 Reference

Figure 8-1   Internetwork with Public IPv4 Addresses

Use public network 128.107.0.0 (Class B).
All interfaces/subnets use a /24 (255.255.255.0) mask.

Subnet 128.107.11.0/24   Subnet 128.107.112.0/24   Subnet 128.107.12.0/24

Figure 8-2   IPv4 Addresses: Network, Subnet, Host, and Prefix Length

Network   Host

Subnet 128.107.11.0/24

Subnet   Prefix
Length

All **addresses in this internetwork** begin with 128.107

All **addresses on this LAN** begin with 128.107.11

The prefix length is the **length of network + subnet**

All addresses on this LAN need a different host ID; the **host ID is shown as 0s** in subnet number

Figure 8-3   IPv6 ISP Prefix

ISP Prefix

Subnet **2233:0000:2222:**0011:0000:0000:0000:0000/64

All **addresses in this internetwork** begin with 2233:0000:2222

Figure 8-4   IPv6 Subnet

Subnet

Subnet 2233:0000:2222:**0011**:0000:0000:0000:0000/64

All **addresses in this internetwork** begin with 2233:0000:2222

All **addresses on this LAN** begin with   2233:0000:2222:0011

Figure 8-5   IPv6 Prefix Length

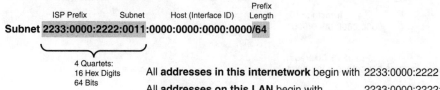

ISP Prefix   Subnet   Host (Interface ID)   Prefix
                                                      Length

Subnet **2233:0000:2222:0011**:0000:0000:0000:0000/**64**

4 Quartets:
16 Hex Digits
64 Bits

All **addresses in this internetwork** begin with 2233:0000:2222

All **addresses on this LAN** begin with   2233:0000:2222:0011

The prefix length is the length of ISP prefix + subnet

All addresses on this LAN need a different interface ID; the **interface ID is shown as 0s** in subnet number

Figure 8-6   IPv6 Host (Interface) ID

ISP Prefix   Subnet   Host (Interface ID)

Subnet 2233:0000:2222:0011:**0000:0000:0000:0000**/64

All **addresses in this internetwork** begin with 2233:0000:2222

All **addresses on this LAN** begin with   2233:0000:2222:0011

The prefix length is the **length of ISP prefix + subnet**

All addresses on this LAN need a different interface ID; the **interface ID is shown as 0s** in subnet number

Figure 8-7   Abbreviating IPv6 Addresses and Subnet Numbers

Subnet 2233:0000:2222:0011:0000:0000:0000:0000/64

Subnet 2233:0000:2222:11:0000:0000:0000:0000/64

Subnet 2233:0:2222:11:0000:0000:0000:0000/64

Subnet 2233:0:2222:11::/64

1) Leading 0s in a quartet can always be omitted
2) A quartet of 0000 can be abbreviated as 0
3) One instance of multiple consecutive 0000 quartets can be abbreviated as ::

Step 2 Reference

Figure 8-8   IPv6 Subnets and Addresses Chosen for This Video

2233:0:2222:11::/64   2233:0:2222:112::/64   2233:0:2222:12::/64

Interface ID:
0000:0000:0000:0001

Full IPv6 Address:
2233:0:2222:11:0000:0000:0000:0001

PPP and CHAP Configuration

This *CCNA Video Mentor* lab shows how to configure Point-to-Point Protocol (PPP) and Challenge Handshake Authentication Protocol (CHAP). The objectives of this lab are as follows:

- Configure PPP

- Describe the meaning of the two interface status codes

- Configure CHAP

- Explain how CHAP does not send the password over the link when performing authentication

Scenario

This lab contains two main steps, as follows:

Step 1.   Migrate from HDLC to PPP

Step 2.   Add CHAP authentication to a PPP link

Initial Configurations

Examples 9-1 and 9-2 show the pertinent initial configurations of routers R1 and R2 in the lab video. The lab begins with a working network, using the default of High-Level Data Link Control (HDLC) as the data link protocol on the serial link. As usual, the parts of the configurations not relevant to this lab have been omitted.

Example 9-1   Initial Configuration for R1

```
hostname R1
!
interface FastEthernet 0/0
 ip address 172.16.1.1 255.255.255.0
!
interface serial 0/1/0
 ip address 172.22.2.1 255.255.255.0
 clock rate 1536000
 shutdown
!
router rip
 network 172.16.0.0
```

Example 9-2   Initial Configuration for R2

```
hostname R2
!
interface FastEthernet 0/0
 ip address 172.16.3.2 255.255.255.0
!
interface serial 0/1/0
 ip address 172.16.2.2 255.255.255.0
!
router rip
 network 172.16.0.0
```

Ending Configurations

This lab ends with both routers having migrated to using PPP and CHAP. Examples 9-3 and 9-4 show the configurations added to R1 and R2 during the lab.

Example 9-3   Configuration Added to R1 During the Lab

```
username R2 password depth
!
interface serial 0/1/0
 no shutdown
 encapsulation ppp
 ppp authentication chap
```

Example 9-4   Configuration Added to R2 During the Lab

```
username R1 password depth
!
interface serial 0/1/0
 encapsulation ppp
 ppp authentication chap
```

Video Presentation Reference

This video includes several figures that contain the same images used in the lab video. Because the video is organized into two separate steps, the reference materials have been organized into two separate sections. Each section simply lists these figures and tables for reference.

Step 1 Reference

Figure 9-1   **Two Routers Using a Point-to-Point Serial Link**

Subnet 172.16.2.0/24

R1
172.16.2.1
S0/1/0
Fa0/0
172.16.1.1

172.16.2.2
S0/1/0
R2
Fa0/0
172.16.3.2

Subnet 172.16.1.0/24

Subnet 172.16.3.0/24

Table 9-1 lists the interface status code combinations and their meanings.

Table 9-1   **Cisco Router Interface Status Code Combinations**

First Interface Status Code	Second Interface Status Code	Most Likely Meaning
Administratively down	Down	Interface has been shut down
Down	Down	Layer 1 problem
Up	Down	Layer 2 problem
Up	Up	Interface is working

Step 2 Reference

Figure 9-2   **Three-way CHAP Authentication Message Flow**

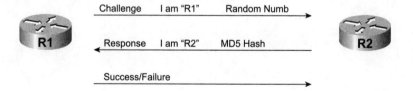

R1

Challenge   I am "R1"   Random Numb

Response   I am "R2"   MD5 Hash

Success/Failure

R2

Figure 9-3   Comparing CHAP Configuration with CHAP Message Flow

Access Lists

This *CCNA Video Mentor* lab shows how to configure access control lists (ACLs), focusing on how ACLs can match applications based on TCP and UDP port numbers. The objectives of this lab are as follows:

- Configure extended IP ACLs

- Describe how to match both the source and destination port numbers with an IP ACL

- See counters for the number of packets that match each ACL statement

Scenario

This lab contains a single step, as follows:

Step 1. Filter packets going to a server farm

Initial Configurations

Examples 10-1 and 10-2 show the pertinent initial configurations of routers R1 and R2 in the lab video. The lab begins with a working network with IP addresses and the RIP routing protocol, but with no ACLs configured. As usual, the parts of the configurations not relevant to this lab have been omitted.

Example 10-1   Initial Configuration for R1

```
hostname R1
!
interface FastEthernet 0/0
 ip address 172.16.1.251 255.255.255.0
!
interface serial 0/1/0
 ip address 172.16.2.251 255.255.255.0
!
router rip
 network 172.16.0.0
```

Example 10-2   Initial Configuration for R2

```
hostname R2
!
interface FastEthernet 0/0
 ip address 172.16.3.252 255.255.255.0
!
interface serial 0/1/0
 ip address 172.16.2.252 255.255.255.0
!
router rip
 network 172.16.0.0
```

Ending Configurations

This lab ends with R1 having a new ACL configured and enabled. Example 10-3 shows the ending configuration for R1.

Example 10-3   Configuration for R1 at the End of the Lab

```
hostname R1
!
interface FastEthernet 0/0
 ip address 172.16.1.251 255.255.255.0
 ip access-group 101 in
!
interface serial 0/1/0
 ip address 172.16.2.251 255.255.255.0
!
router rip
 network 172.16.0.0
!
access-list 101 permit tcp host 172.16.1.1 172.16.3.0 0.0.0.255 eq www
access-list 101 permit tcp 172.16.1.0 0.0.0.255 gt 1023 172.16.3.0 0.0.0.255 eq
telnet
```

Video Presentation Reference

This video includes several figures that contain the same images used in the lab video. Because the video is organized into two separate steps, the reference materials have been organized into two separate sections. Each section simply lists these figures for reference.

Step 1 Reference

Figure 10-1   Lab 12 IP Address Reference

Figure 10-2   Lab 12 Subnet Reference

Figure 10-3   View of Packets That Should be Permitted by the ACL

Permit: from PC1 to web servers in subnet 172.16.3.0/24
Permit: from subnet 172.16.1.0/24 to Telnet servers in subnet 172.16.3.0/24
Deny: all else

Access Lists II

This *CCNA Video Mentor* lab shows how to configure access control lists (ACL), focusing on how ACLs can match applications based on TCP and UDP port numbers. The objectives of this lab are as follows:

- Explain how discarding packets sent by a server to a client prevents a client from talking to a server.

- Configure ACLs to match well-known ports as source ports.

- See counters for the number of packets that match each ACL statement.

Scenario

This lab contains a single step, as follows:

Step 1.   Filter packets coming from a server farm.

Initial Configurations

Example 11-1 and Example 11-2 show the pertinent initial configurations of Routers R1 and R2 in the lab video. The lab begins with a working network with IP addresses and the RIP routing protocol, but with no ACLs configured. As usual, the parts of the configurations not relevant to this lab have been omitted.

Example 11-1   Initial Configuration for R1

```
hostname R1
!
interface FastEthernet 0/0
 ip address 172.16.1.251 255.255.255.0
!
interface serial 0/1/0
 ip address 172.16.2.251 255.255.255.0
!
router rip
 network 172.16.0.0
```

Example 11-2   Initial Configuration for R2

```
hostname R2
!
interface FastEthernet 0/0
 ip address 172.16.3.252 255.255.255.0
!
interface serial 0/1/0
 ip address 172.16.2.252 255.255.255.0
!
router rip
 network 172.16.0.0
```

Ending Configurations

This lab ends with R1 having a new configured and enabled ACL. Example 11-3 shows the ending configuration for R1.

Example 11-3   Configuration for R1 at the End of the Lab

```
hostname R1
!
interface FastEthernet 0/0
 ip address 172.16.1.251 255.255.255.0
 ip access-group 101 in
!
interface serial 0/1/0
 ip address 172.16.2.251 255.255.255.0
!
router rip
 network 172.16.0.0
!
access-list 101 permit tcp 172.16.3.0 0.0.0.255 eq www host 172.16.1.1 gt 1023
access-list 101 permit tcp 172.16.3.0 0.0.0.255 eq telnet 172.16.1.0 0.0.0.255 gt
 1023
access-list 101 deny ip any any
```

Video Presentation Reference

This video includes several figures that contain the same images used in the lab video. Because the video is organized into a single scenario step, the figures are listed in a single section for reference.

Figure 11-1   Lab 11 IP Address Reference

Figure 11-2   Lab 11 Subnet Reference

Figure 11-3   **Lab 11 Filtering Reference**

Permit: PC1 Web Client Communicating with Web Servers in Subnet 172.16.3.0/24
Permit: Telnet Clients in Subnet 172.16.1.0/24 and Telnet Servers in 172.16.3.0/24
Deny All Else

Advances in Waveform-Agile Sensing for Tracking
Sandeep Prasad Sira, Antonia Papandreou-Suppappola, and Darryl Morrell
2008

Despeckle Filtering Algorithms and Software for Ultrasound Imaging
Christos P. Loizou and Constantinos S. Pattichis
2008

Copyright © 2012 by Morgan & Claypool

Analysis of the MPEG-1Layer III (MP3) Algorithm Using MATLAB

Jayaraman J. Thiagarajan and Andreas Spanias

www.morganclaypool.com

ISBN: 9781608458011   paperback
ISBN: 9781608458028   ebook

DOI 10.2200/S00382ED1V01Y201110ASE009

A Publication in the Morgan & Claypool Publishers series
SYNTHESIS LECTURES ON ALGORITHMS AND SOFTWARE IN ENGINEERING

Lecture #9
Series Editor: Andreas Spanias, *Arizona State University*
Series ISSN
Synthesis Lectures on Algorithms and Software in Engineering
Print 1938-1727   Electronic 1938-1735

Analysis of the MPEG-1 Layer III (MP3) Algorithm Using MATLAB

Jayaraman J. Thiagarajan and Andreas Spanias
Arizona State University

SYNTHESIS LECTURES ON ALGORITHMS AND SOFTWARE IN ENGINEERING #9

MORGAN & CLAYPOOL PUBLISHERS

ABSTRACT

The MPEG-1 Layer III (MP3) algorithm is one of the most successful audio The MPEG-1 Layer III (MP3) algorithm is one of the most successful audio formats for consumer audio storage and for transfer and playback of music on digital audio players. The MP3 compression standard along with the AAC (Advanced Audio Coding) algorithm are associated with the most successful music players of the last decade. This book describes the fundamentals and the MATLAB implementation details of the MP3 algorithm. Several of the tedious processes in MP3 are supported by demonstrations using MATLAB® software. The book presents the theoretical concepts and algorithms used in the MP3 standard. The implementation details and simulations with MATLAB® complement the theoretical principles. The extensive list of references enables the reader to perform a more detailed study on specific aspects of the algorithm and gain exposure to advancements in perceptual coding.

KEYWORDS

perceptual audio coders, lossy coding, MPEG standards, psychoacustic models, MP3 algorithm, variable-bit-rate coding

Contents

Preface

The MPEG-1 audio Layer-3, popularly referred to as the MP3, is a digital encoding format based on perceptual audio compression. This audio-specific format, designed by the Moving Pictures Expert Group, was standardized as a part of the generic MPEG-1 standard in the early 1990's. MP3 has found widespread application in consumer audio storage and in recording and playback of music on digital audio players. The MP3 compression standard along with the AAC (Advanced Audio Coding) standard is associated with perhaps the most successful music players of the last decade.

This book presents MATLAB® software that implements several important functions of the MPEG-1 Layer 3 encoding and decoding algorithms. We describe the fundamentals and implementation details of the algorithm along with several MATLAB® demonstrations. In the First chapter, we present a brief discussion on the history of audio coders and describe the architectural overview of perceptual coders. Furthermore, we describe the principles of psychoacoustics and provide details of the *psychoacoustic model I* used in the earlier MPEG audio coders. From Chapter 2 and on, we discuss the various modules of the MP3 algorithm. The theory sections in most chapters provide description of the necessary concepts required to understand the algorithm. The implementation details and simulations with MATLAB® functions complement these descriptions. The extensive list of references will enable the reader to perform a more detailed study on specific aspects of the algorithm and gain exposure to some of the recent advancements in perceptual coding. Finally, a detailed analysis of the computational complexity of the MP3 algorithm, for both the C and MATLAB implementations, is presented

Audio coders, in addition to being an interesting application of signal processing principles for students, present a valuable resource to both practitioners and researchers in several other sound related implementations. In particular, the functions and software provided in this book will enable practitioners and algorithm developers to understand and optimize/modify sections of the algorithm in order to achieve improved performance and design computationally efficient implementations. Furthermore, understanding the principles of the MP3 algorithm will enable the reader to understand and analyze several of the more recent perceptual coders. Students will be able to visualize and understand the various modules of MP3 by using the software and the associated simulations.

Jayaraman J. Thiagarajan and Andreas Spanias
October 2011

Acknowledgments

The authors acknowledge Ramapriya Rangachar, a Masters graduate student that worked in our lab, who was involved in developing some of the MATLAB® code for the MP3 algorithm, and ISO for developing the C code for the algorithm. We note that the MATLAB® code presented in this book is organized in modules by the authors in order to facilitate the learning of the MP3 functions. In fact, several functions have been developed directly from the original standard documentation. The authors also like to thank Ted Painter and Venkatraman Atti for providing descriptions of some of the foundations of psychoacoustics and audio coding. In addition, the first author acknowledges Karthikeyan N. Ramamurthy, Harini Sridhar and Vivek Iyer for their support. Portions of this work and associated software have been supported by the SenSIP Center and NSF grants 0817596, 1035086.

Jayaraman J. Thiagarajan and Andreas Spanias
October 2011

CHAPTER 1

Introduction

Audio coding or *audio compression* algorithms obtain reduced bit rate representations of high-fidelity audio signals and have applications in transmission, storage, streaming and broadcasting. The objective of audio coding algorithms is to represent the signal with a small number of bits while maintaining its perceptual quality such that it is indistinguishable from the original. The compact disk (CD) introduced true high-fidelity at high data rates. Conventional digital audio signals are associated with sampling frequencies of either 44.1 (CD) or 48 kHz (DAT) and the samples are encoded with pulse code modulation (PCM) at 16-bits per sample. This results in very high data rates amounting to 1.41 Mbits/s for a stereo-pair sampled at 44.1 kHz. Motivated by the need for compression algorithms for network and portable applications several codecs have been established. The focus of this book is to present a detailed analysis of several aspects of the MPEG-1 Layer-III audio coding standard. To facilitate the understanding of MP3, the theoretical concepts discussed in the following chapters are accompanied by various simulation examples. Furthermore, this book emphasizes the implementation specifics of the MP3 codec by including MATLAB code snippets and a detailed complexity analysis of the encoder and decoder functions.

1.1 A BRIEF HISTORY OF AUDIO CODERS

Digital audio compression relies on sophisticated time-frequency analysis techniques that use transform coders, filterbanks or hybrid signal-adaptive coding techniques. Audio coding relies heavily on exploiting properties of psychoacoustics [1, 2, 3, 4]. Foundations of audio coding using filter banks have been established both in the time-domain [5, 6, 7, 8, 9, 10, 11, 12, 13] and the frequency domain [14, 15]. Furthermore, Discrete Wavelet Transform (DWT) based subband coders [16, 17, 18] have also been considered for audio coding due to the flexibility in the choice of filter coefficients. The characterization of the auditory filterbank in terms of critical bands [2] has been used in audio compression and over the years several filterbanks [19, 20, 21, 22, 23] have been proposed to mimic the critical band structure. Furthermore, several quantization strategies have also been applied to transform-coders that use the discrete cosine transform (DCT) [24] and the modified DCT (MDCT) [25].

During the early nineties, several workgroups and organizations such as the ISO/IEC and the International Telecommunications Union (ITU) became actively involved in developing perceptual audio coding standards. The Masking pattern adapted Universal Subband Integrated Coding and Multiplexing (MUSICAM) algorithm [20, 26] had an initial influence on the ISO/IEC (International Organization for Standardization/International Electro-technical Commission) MPEG

(Moving Pictures Experts Group) audio standards, i.e., MPEG-1 [27] and the MPEG-2 [28]. Furthermore, several successful commercial audio standards have been published including Sony's Adaptive TRansform Acoustic Coding (ATRAC), DTS Coherent Acoustics (DTS-CA) and Dolby's Audio Coder-3 (AC-3). Elements or entire algorithms for perceptual coding have also appeared in [21, 23], [27, 28, 29, 30, 31, 32, 33, 34, 35, 36, 37, 38, 39, 41, 42, 44, 45, 46, 47, 48, 49, 50, 51, 52, 53]. With the emergence of surround sound systems, multi-channel encoding formats also gained interest [54, 55, 56]. The advent of ISO/IEC MPEG-4 standardization [45, 47] established new research goals for high-quality coding of general audio signals even at low bit rates. MPEG-4 audio encompasses an integrated family of algorithms with wide ranging provisions for scalable, object-based speech and audio coding at bit rates from 200 bps up to 64 kbps per channel [57, 58].

1.1.1   RECENT AUDIO CODECS

The older MPEG-1 hybrid audio coding technique (ISO/IEC 11172-3) incorporates subband filter bank decomposition, signal transforms such as the FFT and psychoacoustic analysis. MPEG-1 audio operates on 16-bit PCM input audio data and accommodates sample rates of 32, 44.1, and 48 kHz. Operating modes of this algorithm include mono, stereo, dual independent mono, and joint stereo. The target bit rates are programmable in the range of 32-192 kbits/s for mono and 64-384 kbits/s for stereo. Despite the fact that MPEG-1 Layer-III (MP3) is still an active and popular standard, several new algorithms have been shown to perform better. Advanced Audio Coding (AAC) is a standardized, lossy compression scheme that generally achieves better sound quality than MP3 at similar bit rates. It has been standardized by the ISO and IEC as part of the MPEG-2 and MPEG-4 standards. Designed as a successor to the MP3 algorithm, AAC allows more sampling frequencies (8 kHz to 96 kHz) and supports up to 48 channels.

Though perceptual audio coders such as the MP3 and AAC offer reasonably good quality at bit rates down to 80 kbps, they are associated with an algorithmic delay that exceeds 120 ms. Applications such as two-way communications or broadcasting require low end-to-end delays of the order of 20 ms. As a result, Low Delay (LD) audio coding schemes have been developed and they provide comparable perceptual quality to MP3 or AAC with a very low algorithmic delay. The MPEG-4 AAC audio coder is used as a basis to build the low delay functionality preferable in end-to-end applications such as teleconferencing and telephony. Typical bit rates of AAC-LD start at 32 kbps for a mono signal with 22 kHz sampling rate and reach 128 kbps providing excellent audio quality [59]. AAC-ELD (Enhanced Low Delay) was standardized as part of MPEG in January 2008. AAC-ELD has an algorithmic delay of 32 ms at 24 kbps down to 15 ms at 64 kbps. AAC-ELD combines the advantages of AAC-LD for low encoding/decoding purposes and Spectral Band Replication (SBR) for preserving high quality at low bit rates. Delay critical applications such as wideband audio/video conferencing, broadcasting which require high quality audio at low bit rates can benefit from this scheme [60]. The Ultra Low Delay (ULD) AAC [61] was developed at Fraunhofer and attains delays of the order of 8 ms.

The need for an interface to exchange multimedia content through the internet resulted in the development of the MPEG-7 audio standard [48]. MPEG-7 supports a broad range of applications [62] that include the following: multimedia indexing/searching, multimedia editing, broadcast media selection, and multimedia digital library sorting. Issues such as the "interoperability" and multimedia resource delivery over a wide range of networks and terminals motivated the MPEG-21 Framework [53].

As mentioned earlier, Adaptive Transform Acoustic Coding (ATRAC) is a family of audio compression algorithms developed by Sony. Though the initial versions of ATRAC were used with the MiniDisc in the early 1990s, today the recent advanced ATRAC algorithms are used in several Sony-branded audio players, the Real Audio 8 and the native audio compression format for audio rendering in PS3 [63]. The MPEG-4 parametric audio codec, called Harmonic and Individual Lines plus Noise (HILN), enables coding of general audio signals at bitrates as low as 4 kbit/s using a parametric representation [64]. The encoder assumes that the audio signals can be synthesized using only sinusoids and noise. The input signal is decomposed into components based on appropriate source models and represented by model parameters. This approach utilizes more advanced source modeling than just assuming a stationary signal for the duration of a frame.

The launch of storage formats (in 1999) such as the DVD-Audio and the Super Audio CD (SACD) provided the audio codec designers with enormous storage capacity. This motivated an effort for *lossless* coding of digital audio [46, 51, 65]. A lossless audio coding system is able to reconstruct perfectly a "bit-for-bit representation" of the original input audio from the coded bitstream. In contrast, a coding scheme incapable of perfect reconstruction from the coded representation is called *lossy*. Several commercially successful lossless codecs have been developed in the last decade. Some of the earliest lossless audio coders include the Apple Lossless Audio Codec (ALAC) [66] and the Windows Media Audio 9 (WMA 9) lossless codec [13]. ALAC is an audio codec developed by Apple Inc. for lossless data compression of digital music. Typically, it is stored within an MP4 container with the filename extension .m4a. Though this extension is also used by AAC, ALAC employs linear prediction similar to other lossless codecs. All current iPod and iPhone devices can play Apple Lossless-encoded files. The WMA 9 lossless codec was released by Microsoft in early 2003 and it supports up to 96 kHz, 24-bit, 5.1 discrete channels with full dynamic range compression control. It can compress this multichannel signal audio CD at bit rates of 470 to 940 kbit/s.

Dolby TrueHD is an advanced lossless multi-channel audio codec developed by Dolby Laboratories [67]. It is primarily intended for high-definition home-entertainment equipment such as the Blu-ray Disc and the HD DVD. Though Dolby TrueHD is based on Meridian Lossless Packing (MLP) [46], it is significantly different from DVD-Audio. This variable bit-rate codec can support up to 14 discrete sound channels in its bitstream. Another important audio codec is DTS-HD Master Audio, developed by Digital Theater System [11]. It is an optional audio format for the Blu-ray Disc format exclusively. This format aims to allow a bit-to-bit representation of the original movie's studio master soundtrack. To accomplish this, DTS-HD MA supports variable bit rates up to 24.5 Mbit/s on a Blu-ray Disc and up to 18.0 Mbit/s for HD DVD. The DTS-HD Master Audio contains 2 data streams: the original DTS core stream and the residual stream which contains the difference between the original signal and the lossy compression DTS core stream [68]. The residual data is then encoded by a lossless encoder and packed together with the core. The most recent version of the Real player also supports lossless coding. The RealAudio lossless codec is designed primarily for high-quality music downloads in mono or two-channel stereo format (multichannel output is not supported). It replicates CD-quality sound in a format that takes less time for the user to download. Although the lossless audio codec is designed for high-fidelity music downloads, it can also be used for broadcasts in high-bandwidth environments.

The MPEG-4 Audio Lossless Coding, also referred as MPEG-4 ALS [12], extends the MPEG-4 Part 3 audio standard to perform lossless audio compression. It comprises of a short-term predictor, which is a quantized LPC predictor with a lossless residual, and a long term predictor modeled by 5 long-term weighted residues, each with its own delay. The long term predictor improves the compression for sounds with rich harmonics found in several musical instruments and human voice.

1.2   A GENERAL PERCEPTUAL AUDIO CODING ARCHITECTURE

It is important to note the architectural similarities that characterize most perceptual audio coders before we describe the MP3 audio codec in the following chapters. Over the last few years, researchers have proposed several efficient signal models and compression standards/methodologies for high-quality digital audio reproduction. Most of these algorithms are based on the generic architecture shown in Figure 1.1. Most coders typically segment input signals into quasi-stationary frames ranging from 2 to 50 ms in duration. This is followed by a time-frequency analysis to estimate the temporal and spectral components of each frame. Often, the time-frequency mapping is matched to the analysis properties of the human auditory system, although this is not always the case. The objective is to extract a set of time-frequency parameters that can be efficiently coded based on perceptual criteria. The time-frequency analysis module can typically comprise of time-invariant or time-varying filterbanks, harmonic analyzers and hybrid transforms.

The choice of time-frequency analysis methodology always involves a fundamental tradeoff between time and frequency resolution requirements. The time-frequency analysis module employed in the MPEG-1 codec is described in Chapter 2 and the strategies to handle the different resolution requirements are presented in Chapter 4. Perceptual distortion control is achieved by a psychoacoustic signal analysis module that estimates signal masking power based on psychoacoustic principles. The psychoacoustic model quantifies the maximum amount of distortion at each point in the time-frequency plane such that quantization of the time-frequency parameters does not introduce audible artifacts. The steps involved in the estimation of the masking thresholds using the psychoacoustic model – II are explained in Section 3.2 of this book. The quantization and encoding module can also exploit statistical redundancies through classical techniques such as DPCM or ADPCM. The redundancies in the quantized parameters can be removed using run-length and entropy coding

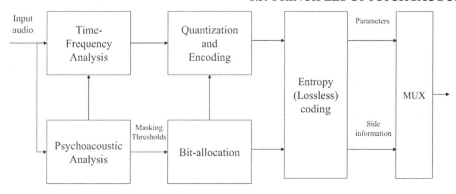

Figure 1.1: A generic block diagram of a perceptual audio encoder.

strategies [69, 70, 71]. Since the psychoacoustic module is signal dependent, most audio coding algorithms are variable rate. However, fixed channel rates can be achieved by efficient management of bit allocation using buffer feedback schemes. The coding methodology and the bit management techniques employed in the MP3 algorithm to achieve a fixed average bit rate are discussed in Sections 5.4 and 5.5, respectively.

1.3   PRINCIPLES OF PSYCHOACOUSTICS

Audio coding algorithms rely on generalized models of human hearing to optimize coding efficiency. The receiver is ultimately the human ear, and sound perception is affected by its masking properties. The field of psychoacoustics has made significant progress toward characterizing the time-frequency analysis capabilities of the inner ear. This, in turn, enabled audio coders to achieve compression by exploiting "irrelevant" information that is not detectable by even a trained listener. Irrelevant information is identified by incorporating psychoacoustic principles in quantization rules, including critical band frequency analysis and masking. The psychoacoustic model described in Chapter 3 relies on the principles discussed in this section. The *Sound Pressure Level* (SPL) is a standard metric that quantifies the intensity of an acoustic stimulus. The SPL provides the level (intensity) of sound pressure in decibels (dB) relative to an internationally defined reference level, i.e., $L_{SPL} = 20 \log_{10}(p/p_0)$, where L_{SPL} is the SPL of a stimulus, p is the sound pressure of the stimulus in Pascals (Pa - equivalent to Newton/m^2), and p_0 is the standard reference level of $20\mu Pa$. Loosely speaking, about 150 dB SPL spans the dynamic range of the auditory system; an SPL reference of a quiet environment is around 0 dB SPL while a stimulus of 140 dB SPL approaches the threshold of pain. The absolute threshold of hearing shown in Figure 1.2 characterizes the amount of energy needed in a pure tone such that it can be detected by a listener in a noiseless environment.

The curve for the absolute threshold of hearing alone cannot be used for audio coding. Typically, music records require spectrally complex quantization rules and hence one has to modify the

Figure 1.2: The absolute threshold of hearing in a noiseless environment.

absolute threshold in a dynamic manner. In order to estimate a time-varying threshold, one must use models for human hearing that take into account how the human ear performs spectral analysis. A frequency-to-place transformation takes place in the cochlea (inner ear), along the basilar membrane [72]. The loudness (perceived intensity) remains constant for a narrowband noise source presented at a constant SPL even as the noise bandwidth is increased up to the critical bandwidth. For any increase beyond the critical bandwidth, the loudness begins to increase. Critical bandwidth tends to remain constant (about 100 Hz) up to 500 Hz, and increases to approximately 20% of the center frequency above 500 Hz. The width of a critical band is commonly referred to as one *Bark*. The nonlinear function,

$$H_z\left(f\right) = 1.3 \arctan\left(0.00076\,f\right) + 3.5 \arctan\left[\left(\frac{f}{7500}\right)^2\right] \text{(Bark)} \tag{1.1}$$

is often used to convert frequency from the Hertz to the Bark scale. Table 1.1 shows the idealized critical band filter bank in terms of band edges and center frequencies for a collection of 26 critical bandwidth auditory filters that span the audio spectrum. The frequency resolution of the auditory filter bank largely determines which portions of a signal are perceptually irrelevant. The auditory time-frequency analysis that occurs in the critical band filter bank induces simultaneous and non-simultaneous masking phenomena that are routinely used by modern audio coders to shape the coding distortion spectrum. As we will discuss in Section 5.1. the perceptual models allocate bits for signal components such that the quantization noise is shaped to exploit the *masking* thresholds for a complex sound.

Masking refers to a process where one sound is rendered inaudible because of the presence of another sound. In audio coding typically we distinguish between only three types of simultaneous

Table 1.1: Band Edges of 26 Critical Bandwidth Auditory Filters that Span the Audio Spectrum.

Band No.	Bandwidth (Hz)	Band No.	Bandwidth (Hz)
1	- 100	14	2000-2320
2	100-200	15	2320-2700
3	200-300	16	2700-3150
4	300-400	17	3150-3700
5	400-510	18	3700-4400
6	510-630	19	4400-5300
7	630-770	20	5300-6400
8	770-920	21	6400-7700
9	920-1080	22	7700-9500
10	1080-1270	23	9500-12000
11	1270-1480	24	12000-15500
12	1480-1720	25	15500-25000
13	1720-2000	26	25000-

masking, namely, *noise-masking-tone* (NMT), *tone-masking-noise* (TMN), and *noise-masking-noise* (NMN). In the NMT scenario shown in Figure 1.3 (a), a narrowband noise with 1 Bark bandwidth masks a tone within the same critical band, provided that the intensity of the masked tone is below a predictable threshold directly related to the intensity, and to a lesser extent, center frequency of the

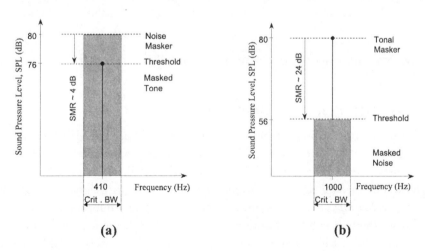

Figure 1.3: (a) Noise masking tone, and (b) tone masking noise [72].

masking noise. In the same figure, a critical band noise masker centered at 410 Hz with an intensity of 80 dB SPL masks a 410 Hz tone. In a tone-masking-noise scenario, Figure 1.3 (b), a 1 kHz pure tone at 80 dB SPL masks a critical band narrowband noise centered at 1 kHz of overall intensity 56 dB SPL. When comparing Figure 1.3 (a) with Figure 1.3 (b), it is important to notice that noise maskers have greater masking power than tonal maskers.

The simultaneous masking effects characterized above by the simplified paradigms of NMT and TMN are not bandlimited to within the boundaries of a single critical band. The effect of a masker centered within one critical band on the psychoacoustic computations in other critical bands is typically modeled by an approximately triangular spreading function that has slopes of +25 dB and -10 dB per bark (Figure 1.4). The global masking threshold or the level of "Just Noticeable Distortion" (JND) is an estimate of level at which the quantization noise becomes perceptible. The standard practice in perceptual coding involves first classifying masking signals as either noise or tone, computing appropriate thresholds, and using this information to shape the noise spectrum beneath the JND level.

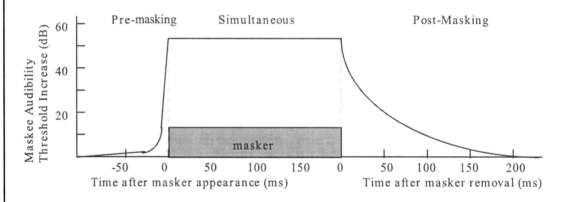

Figure 1.4: Non-simultaneous masking properties of the human ear [72].

1.3.1   PSYCHOACOUSTIC MODEL I

In this section, we briefly discuss the psychoacoustic model I used in MPEG-I audio coders. However, it is important to note that the MP3 algorithm employs a modified version of this model (psychoacoustic model II) and it will be presented in detail in Chapter 3. Researchers in audio coding have combined the notions of psychoacoustic masking with signal quantization principles to define *perceptual entropy* (PE), a measure of perceptually relevant information contained in any audio record. PE is expressed in bits per sample and represents a theoretical limit on the compressibility of a particular signal. PE measurements suggest that a wide variety of CD-quality audio source material can be transparently compressed to approximately 2.1 bits per sample. In psychoacoustics model I, the PE estimation process is accomplished as follows. The signal is windowed (Hanning) and transformed to the frequency domain by a 2048-point Fast Fourier Transform (FFT). Masking thresholds are obtained by performing critical band analysis (with spreading), determining the noise-like or tone-like nature of the signal, applying threshold rules for the signal quality, and then accounting for the absolute hearing threshold. Finally, a determination of the number of bits required to quantize the spectrum without injecting perceptible noise is made. The PE measurement is obtained by constructing a PE histogram over many frames and then choosing a worst-case value as the actual measurement. The details of this psychoacoustic model can be found in [72]. As we will describe in Section 3.2, the ideas for performing the PE computation are embedded in the MP3 codec.

1.4   THE MPEG-1 LAYER III ALGORITHM

The architecture of the MP3 encoder, shown in Figure 1.5, operates on frames that consist of 1152 audio samples; each frame is split into two 576-sample subframes called *granules*. At the decoder,

Figure 1.5: The ISO/MPEG-1 Layer III (MP3) encoder.

every granule can be decoded independently. A hybrid filter bank is used to approximate the critical band model for human hearing. This filter bank includes adaptive segmentation and consists of subband filters followed by the Modified Discrete Cosine Transform (MDCT). The filter bank and MDCT perform time-frequency analysis with adaptive resolution. The filter bank consists of thirty-two channels with fixed bandwidth followed by an MDCT. The MDCT and its software implementation can be found in Chapter 4. The MDCT operates on an adaptive frame length to allow low and high resolution spectral analysis. Sophisticated bit allocation strategies that rely upon non-uniform quantization and entropy coding are used to reduce the overall bit rate and "pack" an audio data record efficiently in a small file. Bit allocation and quantization of the spectral MDCT components are realized in a nested loop procedure that uses both non-uniform quantization and Huffman coding.

1.4.1   ANALYSIS SUBBAND FILTERBANK

As an alternative to tree-structured QMF filter banks, cosine modulation of a lowpass prototype filter is used in the MP3 algorithm to realize the parallel M-channel filter bank. Because these filters do not achieve perfect reconstruction, they are known as pseudo-QMF (PQMF) and are characterized by several attractive properties, i.e., linear phase channel response, constant group delay, low complexity, and fast block realization. In the PQMF bank formulation, phase distortion is eliminated by forcing the k-th analysis and synthesis filters to satisfy the mirror image condition on their L-th order impulse responses. Moreover, adjacent channel aliasing is cancelled by establishing precise relationships between the analysis and synthesis filters.

1.4.2   MDCT AND HYBRID FILTER BANK

The filter bank outputs are processed using the MDCT. The data is segmented and processed with 50% overlapping blocks. In Layer III, there are two possible block sizes for the MDCT, namely, a short block (12 samples) and a long block (36 samples). The MDCT module employs short blocks (better time resolution) for quick transients and long blocks (better frequency resolution) for slowly varying signals. The selection of long and short blocks, based on the perceptual entropy measure, is described in Section 4.2. To avoid rapid transitions, intermediate long-to-short and short-to-long transition windows are provided in the standard. For a particular block of data, all the filter bank channels can have the same MDCT block-type (short or long) or a mixed mode, where the two lower frequency subbands have long blocks while the remaining 30 upper bands have short blocks. The mixed mode provides better frequency resolution for the lower frequencies while maintaining a high time resolution for the higher frequencies.

1.4.3   PSYCHOACOUSTIC ANALYSIS

As described earlier, the signal analysis modes of the hybrid filter bank and the subsequent quantization rules are determined based on the principles of psychoacoustics. The MP3 psychoacoustic model II determines the maximum allowable quantization noise energy in each critical band such that quantization noise remains inaudible. In one of its modes, the model uses a 512-point FFT for high resolution spectral analysis (86.13 Hz resolution), then estimates individual simultaneous masking thresholds for each input frame due to the presence of tone-like and noise-like maskers in the signal spectrum. A global masking threshold is then estimated for a subset of the original 256 FFT bins by an additive combination of the tonal and individual non-tonal masking thresholds.

1.4.4   BIT ALLOCATION

The bit allocation process uses the parameters estimated in the psychoacoustic module to determine the number of bits to be allocated to each of the subbands. In the MP3 algorithm, a nested loop procedure is implemented which adjusts the quantizer step sizes until the number of bits required to encode the transform components falls within the available bit budget. This is achieved by evaluating the quality of the encoded signal in terms of quantization noise relative to the masked thresholds. Although this audio coding algorithm supports a fixed rate, the bit rates required for each frame is in general time varying. The number of bits provided to each frame is determined within the iteration loop. In Section 5.5.1, we describe a short-term buffer technique, referred to as the bit reservoir, that enhances the coding efficiency by storing surplus bits during periods of low demand and allocating them during periods of high demand. This results in a time-varying instantaneous bit rate but a fixed average bit rate.

1.5   SUMMARY

This chapter provided a review on the history of audio coding algorithms and introduced the general architecture of perceptual audio coders. In addition, we presented a brief discussion on the basic psychoacoustic principles and the implementation of psychoacoustic model-I used in MPEG coders. A more detailed review of the modern audio coding algorithms can be found in the book by Spanias et al. [72]. From Chapter 2 and on, we will present the details of the MPEG-1 Layer III algorithm and provide relevant MATLAB program for all the pertinent functions. Chapter 2 will describe the design of the analysis subband filterbank and analyze the characteristics in terms of its relevance to the human auditory system. The estimation of the masking thresholds and JND using the psychoacoustic model II are discussed in detail in Chapter 3. The principles of the modified DCT and the application of different windows to achieve time-varying temporal and spectral resolutions are detailed in Chapter 4. Chapter 5 illustrates the bit allocation process, quantization and coding of the spectral lines, and the final chapter presents the design of the MP3 decoder for a single channel case.

CHAPTER 2

Analysis Subband Filter Bank

2.1 DESCRIPTION

The MPEG-1 audio codec uses a time-frequency analysis block to extract parameters from the time-domain input signal that are suitable for quantization and encoding based on perceptual criteria. One of the most commonly used tools for time-frequency mapping is a filter bank, which divides the signal spectrum into multiple frequency subbands. In the MPEG-1 audio encoder, the input audio stream is passed through a filter bank that divides the audio input into 32 uniformly spaced frequency subbands. The time-frequency mapping provided by the filter bank is amenable to perceptual noise shaping at the encoder [73]. Furthermore, decomposition of the signal into its constituent frequency components reduces the redundancy in the signal.

The analysis subband filter bank consists of a polyphase structure and is common to all layers of the MPEG-1 audio compression [72]. The filter bank is based on a cosine-modulated lowpass prototype filter and consists of M channels with uniform bandwidth (M=32). This pseudo-QMF (PQMF) filter bank achieves nearly perfect reconstruction [74, 75]. These filter banks can be easily understood using an analysis-synthesis framework as shown in Figure 2.1, which illustrates a uniform 32-band critically sampled analysis-synthesis filter bank. The analysis and synthesis filters are designed suitably to reduce aliasing and imaging distortions.

2.2 CHARACTERISTICS OF THE ANALYSIS FILTER BANK

Efficient coding performance of a perceptual coder depends on the match between the properties of the designed filter bank and the characteristics of the input signal [76]. The filter bank used in the MP3 encoder is critically sampled or maximally decimated, i.e., the number of subband samples is same as the number of input samples. For every 32 input samples, the filter bank produces 32 output samples. In effect, each of the 32 subband filters subsamples its output by a factor of 32. The filters provide good time resolution with a reasonable frequency resolution. A cosine modulated pseudo-QMF M-band filter bank has a nearly perfect reconstruction and has uniform, linear phase channel responses [77]. The prototype impulse response contains 512 samples, with sidelobe suppression better than 96-dB in the stop-band and the output ripple is less than 0.07 dB [27].

Though the analysis subband filterbank has very good characteristics, the lack of sharp cutoff frequencies in the subband filters can cause the spectral component of a tone to leak into an adjacent subband. Since it is impossible to achieve perfectly separated magnitude responses with bandpass filters, there is unavoidable aliasing between the decimated subband samples. As seen in Figure 2.5, there is a significant overlap in the magnitude responses of adjacent bands. To illustrate this effect,

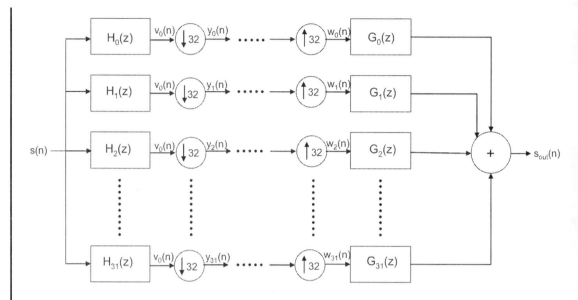

Figure 2.1: A uniform 32-band critically sampled analysis-synthesis filter bank.

consider a single tone of 1500 Hz, provided as an input to this filterbank. The bandwidth of each subband filter is around 689 Hz. Therefore, ideally, the spectral component of the tone should be seen only in subband 3. But due to the overlapping, the tone leaks into the adjacent band (subband 2) also. Figure 2.2 illustrates the input tone and the responses of the two subbands. Furthermore, the subsampling step also introduces aliasing. Hence, alias reduction is performed in the MDCT module, which will be described in Chapter 4.

The other important consideration with this analysis filter bank design is that, the equal widths of the subbands do not reflect the human auditory system's frequency dependent behavior. The width of a *critical band* as a function of frequency is a better indicator of the human auditory behavior [73]. Many psychoacoustic effects are consistent in a critical-band frequency scale. At lower frequencies, a single subband covers several critical bands and in this circumstance the number of quantization bits cannot be allocated for the individual critical bands. Filter banks that emulate the properties of the human auditory system have proven to be highly efficient in coding transient signals. However, such filter banks have been less effective on harmonically structured signals because of their low coding gain compared to filter banks with a large number of subbands. Furthermore, the filter bank and its inverse do not comprise a lossless transformation. Even in the absence of quantization, the inverse transform cannot recover the original signal perfectly. However, by efficient design the error introduced by the filter bank can be made small and inaudible.

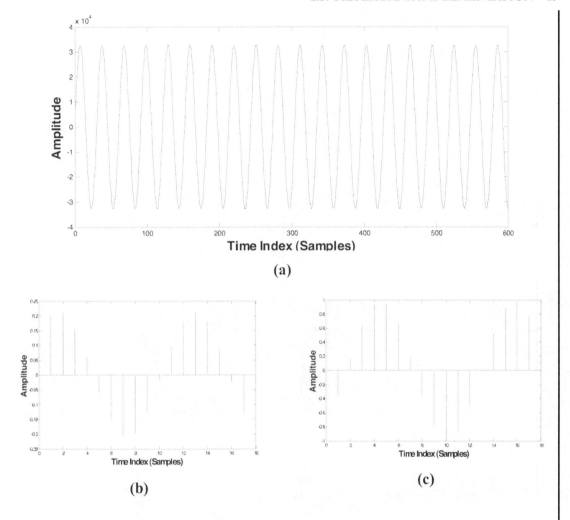

Figure 2.2: (a) Input – single tone of 1500 Hz, (b) Output of subband 2, (c) Output of subband 3.

2.3   FILTER BANK IMPLEMENTATION

The block diagram in Figure 2.3 illustrates the basic steps involved in the implementation of the pseudo-QMF polyphase filter bank. These filter banks are characterized by low-complexity implementations and can be efficiently employed using fast algorithms.

By combining the steps shown in Figure 2.3, the filter bank outputs can be derived as

$$s_i = \sum_{k=0}^{63} \sum_{j=0}^{7} \mathbf{M}_{ik} \left(\mathbf{c} \left(k + 64j \right) \mathbf{x} \left(k + 64j \right) \right) \qquad (2.1)$$

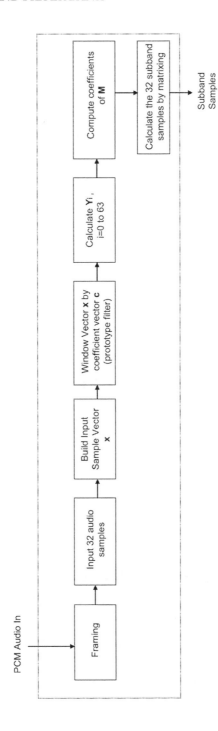

Figure 2.3: Implementation of the analysis subband filterbank.

where i is the subband index and ranges from 0 to 31, $\mathbf{c}$ contains the analysis window coefficients, $\mathbf{x}$ is the audio input sample vector, and $\mathbf{M}$ is a 32×64 matrix with the analysis coefficients, computed as follows.

$$\mathbf{M}_{i,k} = \cos \left[\frac{(2i+1)(k-16)\pi}{64} \right], i = 0 \text{ to } 31, \ k = 0 \text{ to } 63 \ . \tag{2.2}$$

In (2.2), the index i indicates the subband number. It can be observed that (2.1) can be easily reformulated into a familiar filter convolution expression,

$$s_i(n) = \sum_{m=0}^{511} x(n-m) \, h_i^c(m) \ , \tag{2.3}$$

where $x(n)$ is an audio sample at time n, and in this form each subband of the filter bank has its own bandpass filter response, $h_i^c(n)$. Although this form is more convenient for analysis, it is not efficient for implementation. Each of the filters in the polyphase filter bank in (2.3) has a modulated impulse response, i.e.,

$$h_i^c(n) = h(n) \cos \left[\frac{(2i+1)(n-16)\pi}{64} \right], i = 0 \text{ to } 31, \ n = 0 \text{ to } 511 \ . \tag{2.4}$$

The coefficients of the prototype filter, $c(n)$, relate to the impulse response, $h(n)$, as follows.

$$h(n) = \begin{cases} -c(n), & \text{if } \left\lfloor \frac{n}{64} \right\rfloor \text{ is odd} & n = 0 \text{ to } 512 \\[2mm] c(n), & \text{else} & n = 0 \text{ to } 512 \end{cases} . \tag{2.5}$$

The coefficients, $h(n)$, correspond to the prototype lowpass filter response of the polyphase filter bank. Figure 2.4 compares the plots of $c(n)$ with $h(n)$, while Figure 2.5 illustrates the magnitude responses of all 32 subbands of the polyphase filter bank. The $c(n)$ used in (2.1) has every odd-numbered group of 64 coefficients of $h(n)$ negated, so as to compensate for M_{ik}. The cosine term in (2.2) ranges from $k = 0$ to 63 and covers an odd number of half cycles, whereas the cosine term in (2.3) ranges from $n = 0$ to 511 and hence covers eight times the number of half cycles.

The expression for $h_i^c(n)$ in (2.4) clearly indicates that the response of each subband is a modulated version of the prototype response, with a cosine term to shift the lowpass response to the appropriate frequency band. The center frequencies of these filters are at odd multiples of $\pi/(64T)$, where T is the audio sampling period and each has a bandwidth $\pi/(32T)$.

As seen in Figure 2.5, the prototype filter response does not have a sharp cutoff. Furthermore, when the filter outputs are sub-sampled by a factor 32 (for critical sampling), a considerable amount of aliasing occurs. The steps involved in the calculation of the polyphase components and the implementation of the subband filters are described here.

(a)   (b)

Figure 2.4: Coefficients of the prototype filter (a) $c(n)$ and (b) $h(n)$.

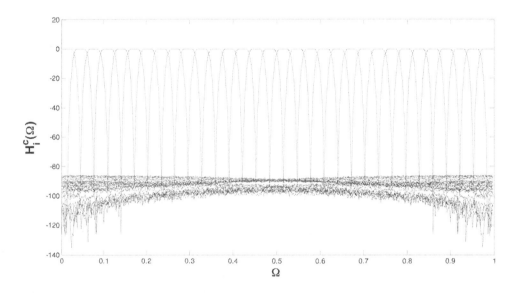

Figure 2.5: Composite magnitude responses of all subbands.

2.3.1 FRAMING

In this algorithm, the input audio is processed in frames of 1152 samples per audio channel. A granule is a group of 576 samples, i.e., half a frame of the input audio data. The subband analysis function takes one frame of the data as input (1152 samples) and produces two granules of 576 frequency lines each. Each granule is then split into 32 subbands with 18 samples in each. As seen in Program 2.1, the input variable to the function, *data*, is of size 2×1152, containing one frame of audio data for each channel. The outer *for* loop indexes the granules, while the inner *for* loop indexes over the channel number. The output variable is a 4-dimensional array $S(ch, gr, sb, samp)$, where ch refers to the channel, gr indicates the granule, sb denotes the subband number and $samp$ contains the 18 samples for each subband.

2.3.2   BUILD INPUT SAMPLE VECTOR

An input sample vector of 512 elements is built using the 32 input audio samples. The most recently acquired 32 samples are inserted into the vector **x** at indices 0 to 31 and the oldest 32 samples shifted out of the vector **x**. This is done to ensure that the first 32 samples of the vector **x** contain the most recent audio samples. The vector $\mathbf{x} = [x_0, x_1 ...., x_{511}]^T$ is updated as

$$x_i = x_{i-32}, \quad i = 511, 510, ..., 32, \tag{2.6}$$
$$x_i = w_{31-i}, \quad i = 31, 30, ..., 0 . \tag{2.7}$$

```
% P 2.1 - Build the input sample vector for subband analysis
function S = SubbandAnalysis(data, channels)
global SBLIMIT HAN_SIZE x C M SCALE;
% Structure of the output - Subband samples
S = zeros(2, 2, 32, 18);

% initial data offset ...
gr_offset = 0;s


% SBLIMIT = 32, HAN_SIZE = 512
for gr = 1:2 % Number of Granules
  for ch = 1:channels % Number of Channels
    for iter = 0:17 % 18 iterations
     % Replace 32 oldest samples with 32 new samples
     x(ch, HAN_SIZE:-1:SBLIMIT+1) = x(ch, HAN_SIZE-SBLIMIT:-1:1);
     x(ch, SBLIMIT:-1:1) = data(ch, gr_offset+iter*SBLIMIT+1:gr_offset...
                     +(iter+1)*SBLIMIT)/SCALE;
```

Program 2.1: MATLAB Code for Building the Input Sample Vector.

2.3.3   WINDOW VECTOR X

The input sample vector $\mathbf{x}$ is windowed by the vector $\mathbf{c}$, which contains the coefficients of the prototype filter. The 512 coefficients of the lowpass prototype filter are plotted in Figure 2.4 and the values can be found in the file *analysis_window.m*. Figure 2.6 illustrates the sample input vector $\mathbf{x}$, impulse response of the window $\mathbf{c}$ and the windowed output vector $\mathbf{z}$. The relation between $\mathbf{x}$, $\mathbf{c}$ and $\mathbf{z}$ can be expressed as,

$$z_i = c_i x_i, i = 0 \text{ to } 511 , \tag{2.8}$$

where, z_i, x_i and c_i are the elements of the vectors $\mathbf{z}$, $\mathbf{x}$ and $\mathbf{c}$, respectively.

```
% P 2.2 - Window Vector X by C
z = zeros(HAN_SIZE, 1);
z = x(ch, 1:HAN_SIZE).*C;
```

Program 2.2: MATLAB Code for Windowing Vector x.

2.3.4   CALCULATION OF THE COSINE MODULATION MATRIX

The cosine modulation filter bank, represented by a 32×64 matrix $\mathbf{M}$, is used to calculate the 32 subband samples. Program 2.3 shows the MATLAB code to compute the cosine modulation matrix.

```
% P 2.3 - Compute coefficients for the matrix M of size 32x64
% Cosine-Modulated Filter bank
M = zeros(32, 64);
for i = 0:31
    for k = 0:63
        M(i+1, k+1) = cos((2*i+1)*(16-k)*pi/64);
    end
end
```

Program 2.3: MATLAB Code for computing M.

Figure 2.6: (a) Sample input vector x, (b) Impulse response of the window, (c) Windowed output vector z.

2.3.5   CALCULATION OF THE SUBBAND SAMPLES

The two steps involved in the computation of the 32 subband samples are shown below.

$$y(i) = \sum_{j=0}^{7} z(i + 64j), \quad i = 0 \text{ to } 63, \tag{2.9}$$

$$s_i = \sum_{k=0}^{63} M_{i,k} y(k), \quad i = 0 \text{ to } 31. \tag{2.10}$$

```
% P 2.4 - Calculation of the output Y
y = zeros(1, 64);
for i = 1:64
  y(i) = sum(z(i:64:HAN_SIZE));
end
% Calculate the 32 subband samples
for i = 1:SBLIMIT
  S(ch, gr, i, iter+1) = sum(y.*M(i, 1:64));
end
```

Program 2.4: MATLAB Code for computing subband samples.

2.4 DEMONSTRATION WITH TEST DATA

Figure 2.7 illustrates the impulse responses and magnitude responses of three different subbands. The output **S** contains 32 subbands with 18 samples in each subband.

2.5 SUMMARY

In this chapter, we described the design and implementation of the subband analysis filter bank used in the MPEG-1 Layer III encoder. It was observed that this filter bank does not reflect the frequency dependent behavior of the human auditory system. The PCM audio signal is divided into 32 subbands by passing it through a filter bank and decimating the output signals by a factor of 32. Since it is not possible to construct filters with perfectly flat responses, aliasing effects can be introduced during the decimation process and these result in some information loss. As evident from the impulse response of the subbands, the subband filter functions do not have a linear phase. However, the cascade of the analysis and synthesis filters for each subband channel is a linear phase filter [78]. Therefore, the entire filter bank is of linear phase and the aliasing will only result in amplitude distortion. Though the aliasing errors of the filters appear substantial from the frequency responses, they are reduced substantially during reconstruction. The reader is referred to [7, 79, 80, 81, 82, 83, 84, 85] for further details on filter banks and their design.

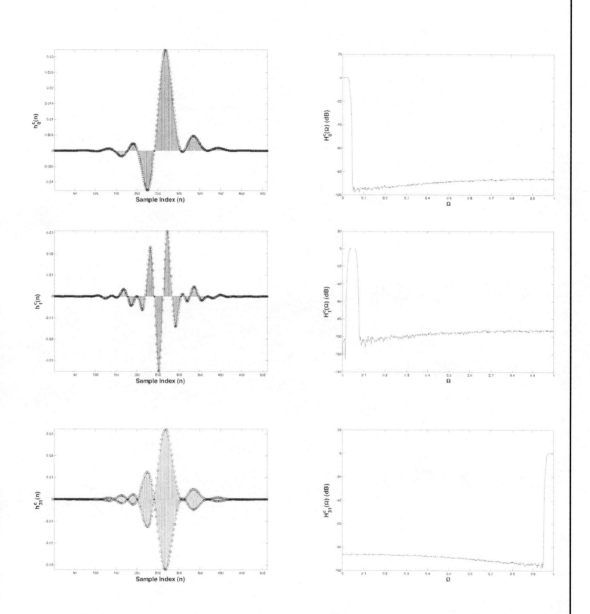

Figure 2.7: Time domain and Frequency responses of the filter bank. Subbands 0,1 and 31 are shown, respectively.

CHAPTER 3

Psychoacoustic Model II

3.1 DESCRIPTION

The MPEG-I psychoacoustic model plays a central role in the compression algorithm. This module produces a time-adaptive spectral pattern that emulates the sensitivity of the human sound perception system. The MPEG audio coder compresses the audio data by removing its perceptually irrelevant components. This is done by exploiting the auditory masking characteristics. The psychoacoustic module analyzes the signal, and computes the noise and signal masking as a function of frequency. The masking characteristics of a given signal component depend on its frequency location and its intensity. The encoder estimates a masking threshold for each subband, below which an audio signal cannot be perceived by the average human listener [86]. The encoder uses this information to determine the best representation of a signal with the limited number of bits. Furthermore, it calculates an estimate of the Perceptual Entropy (PE) which is used to make window-switching decisions [87]. The computation of the masking thresholds and the PE is described in the following sections. The block diagram in Figure 3.1 illustrates the basic steps involved in the psychoacoustic model II as used in the Layer III algorithm.

3.2 ILLUSTRATION OF THE PSYCHOACOUSTIC MODEL II WITH MATLAB CODE

3.2.1 ANALYSIS

The calculation of masking threshold involves the critical band analysis of the signal. Hence, the power spectrum of the signal, which is computed from the complex FFT spectrum of the signal, needs to be partitioned into *critical bands*. The cochlear filter pass bands are of non-uniform bandwidth and the bandwidths increase with increasing frequency. The *critical bandwidth* is a function of frequency that quantifies the cochlear filter bandwidths. For an average listener, the critical bandwidth can be approximated by [73, 88]

$$BW_c(f) = 25 + 75 \left[1 + 1.4\,(f/1000)^2\right]^{0.69} \text{ (Hz)}. \tag{3.1}$$

Table 1.1 shows an idealized filter bank and Figure 3.2 illustrates the corresponding magnitude responses.

The psychoacoustic module needs to account for the delay of the filter bank and for an offset in order to center the data in the audio frame within the psychoacoustic analysis window [27]. This model uses an independent time-to-frequency mapping instead of the polyphase filter bank because

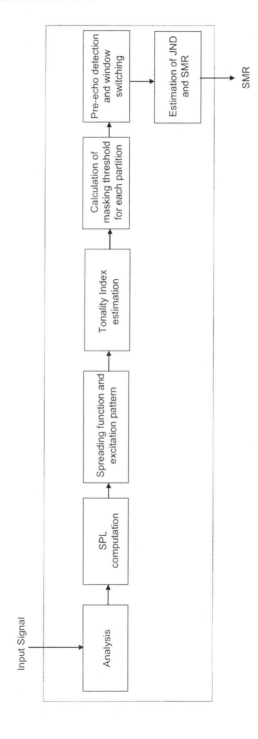

Figure 3.1: Overview of the psychoacoustic model II.

Figure 3.2: Idealized critical band filter bank.

calculation of the masking thresholds requires a finer frequency resolution. The psychoacoustic model II uses the FFT for this mapping. A Hanning window is applied to the audio data, prior to the Fourier transformation, to reduce the edge effects of the transform window. The size of an audio frame in the MPEG-1 algorithm is 1152 samples and the size of the analysis window in the case of long windows is 1024 samples [89]. It can be easily seen that the analysis window cannot cover the frame completely. Hence, Layer III performs two psychoacoustic computations per frame. The first computation deals with the first half of the 1152 samples centered in the analysis window and the other computation deals with the second half. The module finally combines the results of the two calculations and chooses the higher of the two signal-to-mask ratios for each subband. This in effect selects the lower of the two noise masking thresholds for each subband.

The frame size of 1152 samples (32 subbands*36 samples) ensures a frequency resolution of about 41.66 Hz at the sampling rate of 48 kHz. The drawback of this approach is that the quantization errors can be spread over a block of 1152 time samples. In signals containing sharp transients, this results in unmasked temporal noise and pre-echo. Therefore, the Layer III filter bank switches to a higher time resolution to avoid this artifact. During transients, Layer III uses a shorter block size of 384 samples (32 subbands*12 samples), thereby reducing the temporal spreading of the quantization noise. The psychoacoustic model II can choose between long windows of 1024 samples and short windows of 256 samples for analysis. As described earlier, the psychoacoustic model is calculated twice with a delay of 576 samples and the largest of each pair of signal to mask ratios is used. One computation is done with a delay of 192 samples to the audio data, while the other computation is carried out with a delay of 576 samples. In the former case, short windows of 256 samples are used. The analysis stage involves windowing of the time-aligned audio samples, using a Hanning window.

```
% P 3.1 - Spectral Analysis

% flush=576 ; sync_flush=768
% Delay signal by sync_flush=768 samples
delaybuffer(chn,1:sync_flush)=delaybuffer(chn,...
1+flush:sync_flush+flush);

% It is important to note which part of the data is inserted
buf_idx_start = (gr-1)*576+1;
delaybuffer(chn, sync_flush+1:sync_size) = ...
    PCMaudio(chn, buf_idx_start:buf_idx_start+flush-1);
Psycho.InputData = delaybuffer(chn, 1:BLKSIZE);

% Window data with Hanning window
waudio = window.*delaybuffer(chn, 1:BLKSIZE);
```

Program 3.1: MATLAB Code for spectral analysis in the Psychoacoustic module.

Figure 3.3 (a) illustrates the time-aligned input data to the psychoacoustic module for granule 1, while Figure 3.3 (b) shows the output after windowing the data with a Hanning window.

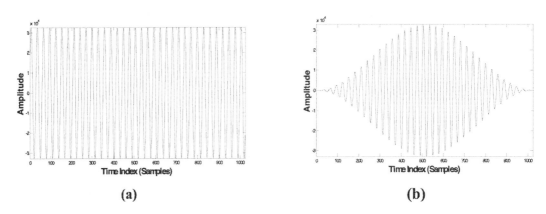

(a)   (b)

Figure 3.3: (a) Time-aligned input data, (b) after applying a Hanning window.

3.2.2   COMPUTATION OF ENERGY AND UNPREDICTABILITY IN THRESHOLD PARTITIONS

The important step involved in this module is to identify the tone-like and noise-like components in the audio signal. The masking abilities of these two components vary considerably [90, 91].

However, the psychoacoustics model II never actually separates completely the tonal and non-tonal components. Instead, it computes a likelihood measure known as the *tonality index* which determines if the component is more tone-like or noise-like. This index measure is estimated as a function of predictability of the spectral components in the current analysis window. In general, tonal components are more predictable than the broadband signals and they exhibit different masking characteristics [92]. Hence, the unpredictability measure of each spectral component is computed in this module, using the complex spectra of the time-aligned and the windowed audio data. The module uses data from two previous analysis windows to predict the components in the current window. A measure of unpredictability is given by,

$$
cw(f) = \frac{\sqrt{\left[\begin{array}{l}\left(R_j(f)\cos(\phi_j(f)) - \hat{R}_j(f)\cos(\hat{\phi}_j(f))\right)^2 + \\ \left(R_j(f)\sin(\phi_j(f)) - \hat{R}_j(f)\sin(\hat{\phi}_j(f))\right)^2\end{array}\right]}}{\left(R_j(f) + \left|\hat{R}_j(f)\right|\right)}
\tag{3.2}
$$

where

$$
\hat{R}_j(f) = 2R_{j-1}(f) - R_{j-2}(f),
$$
$$
\hat{\phi}_j(f) = 2\phi_{j-1}(f) - \phi_{j-2}(f).
$$

Here, $R_j(f)$ denotes the magnitude and $\hat{R}_j(f)$ represents the predicted magnitude of the complex spectrum in the current threshold calculation block. It can be seen that $\hat{R}_j(f)$ is calculated from the complex spectra of the two previous blocks. The index j denotes the current block and the indices $j - 1$ and $j - 2$ index the data in the two previous blocks.

Computing the unpredictability measure for all the spectral lines up to 20 kHz would require a large number of computations. Hence, in this model, the computation is performed only for the first 206 lines and a constant value of 0.4 is set to the remaining spectral lines. The unpredictability of the first 6 lines is calculated using a long FFT (window length=1024), while that of the remaining spectral lines up to 205 is computed using a short FFT block (window length=256).

$$
cw(f) = \begin{cases} c_l(f) & \text{for } 0 \le f < 6 \\ c_s\left(\dfrac{f+2}{4}\right) & \text{for } 6 \le f < 206 \\ 0.4 & \text{for } f \ge 206 \end{cases},
\tag{3.3}
$$

where $c_l(f)$ and $c_s(f)$ are the unpredictability measures computed using the long FFT and short FFT, respectively. The MATLAB code section in 3.2 illustrates the computation of the unpredictability measure. Figure 3.4 (a) shows the FFT magnitude spectrum of the windowed audio data in Figure 3.3(b). The unpredictability measure of the frequency lines is illustrated in Figure 3.4 (b).

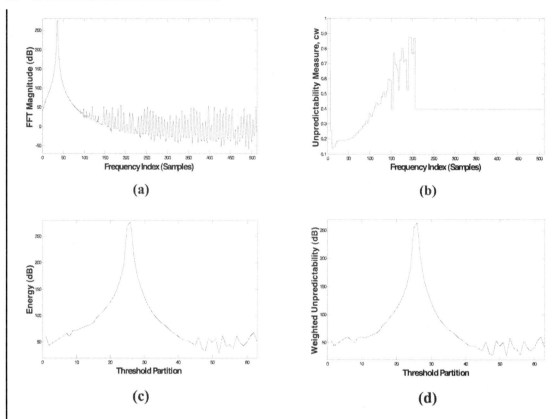

Figure 3.4: (a) FFT magnitude of the windowed audio data, (b) Unpredictability measure (*cw*), (c) Energy of threshold partitions (*eb*), (d) Weighted unpredictability of threshold partitions (*cb*).

It can be clearly seen that the dominant frequency components in the spectrum have a very low unpredictability measure.

To simplify the psychoacoustic calculations, the module processes the frequency lines in the perceptual domain. In model II, the spectral lines are grouped into *threshold calculation partitions*, whose widths are roughly 1/3 of a critical band or one FFT line, whichever is wider at that frequency location. At low frequencies, a single line of the FFT constitutes a single partition whereas many lines are combined into a single calculation partition at higher frequencies. The total number of partitions depends on the choice of the sampling rate. For each threshold partition, the energy is derived using the sum of energy densities in the partition. The energy in each threshold partition is given by

$$eb(z) = \sum_{f=bl_z}^{bh_z} R^2(f),$$

(3.4)

where bl_z and bh_z denote the lower and higher frequency limits of the zth critical band. The weighted unpredictability of each partition is given by,

$$cb(z) = \sum_{f=bl_z}^{bh_z} R^2(f)cw(f),$$

(3.5)

where $cw(f)$ is the unpredictability measure from (3.2). Figure 3.4 (c) and (d) illustrate the energy and weighted unpredictability in the threshold partitions, respectively. It can be seen from Figure 3.4 (c) that the perceptual transformation (mapping) expands the low frequency regions and compresses the high frequency regions. Since cb weights the unpredictability measure cw by the energy in each partition, the weighted unpredictability looks similar to the energy in the partition.

3.2.3   SPREADING FUNCTION AND EXCITATION PATTERN

A strong signal component reduces the audibility of weaker components in the same critical band and also the neighboring bands. Hence, the masking ability of a given signal spreads across its neighboring critical bands also [93, 94]. The psychoacoustic module emulates this by applying a *spreading function* to spread the energy of a critical band across other bands. The total masking energy of the audio frame is derived from the convolution of the spreading function with each of the maskers. This is carried out by spreading the energy of each masker in frequency and computing the sum of relative energies. The spreading function (measured in dB) used in this module is given by [95]

$$\begin{aligned} B(dz) =& 15.8111389 + 7.5 * (a * dz + 0.474) - 17.5 * \sqrt{1.0 + (a * dz + .474)^2} \\ &+ 8 * \min\left(0, (a * dz - 0.5)^2 - 2(a * dz - 0.5)\right), \end{aligned}$$

(3.6)

where dz is the bark distance between the maskee and the masker and

$$a = \begin{cases} 3 & \text{for } dz \geq 0 \\ 1.5 & \text{else} \end{cases}.$$

(3.7)

It is important to note that the model uses only values of the spreading function greater than 60 dB.

$$spf(i, j) = \begin{cases} 0.0 & B(dz) <= -60 \\ 10^{\frac{(x+B(dz))}{10}} & \text{else} \end{cases}.$$

(3.8)

```
% P 3.2 - Compute unpredictability measure in the threshold partitic
% complex FFT
fft_waudio = fft(waudio, 1024 ); % long FFT
energy = abs(fft_waudio).^2;
phi = angle(fft_waudio);

% Calculate unpredictability measure cw
for j = 1:6
    r_prime = 2.0 * r(chn, old, j) - r(chn, oldest, j);
    phi_prime = 2.0 * phi_sav(chn, old, j) - phi_sav(chn, oldest, j);
    r(chn, new, j) = sqrt(energy(j));
    phi_sav(chn, new, j) = phi(j);
    temp1 = r(chn, new, j) * cos(phi(j)) - r_prime * cos(phi_prime);
    temp2 = r(chn, new, j) * sin(phi(j)) - r_prime * sin(phi_prime);
    temp3 = r(chn, new, j) + abs(r_prime);

    if temp3 ~= 0.0
        cw(j) = sqrt( temp1*temp1+temp2*temp2 ) / temp3;
    else
        cw(j) = 0;
    end
end

% Compute unpredictability of the next 200 spectral lines
for sblock = 1:3
    % window data with HANN window
    k = 128 * (2 + sblock-1);
    waudio(1:BLKSIZE_s) = window_s.*delaybuffer(chn, k:k+BLKSIZE_s-1

    % short FFT
    fft_waudio = fft(waudio, 256);
    energy_s(sblock, :) = abs(fft_waudio).^2;
    phi_s(sblock, :) = angle(fft_waudio);
end

sblock = 1;
```

Program 3.2: MATLAB Code for computing unpredictability measure. (*Continues.*)

```matlab
% Calculate unpredictability measure cw
for j = 7:4:206
    k = (j+1)/4 ;
    r_prime = 2.0 * sqrt(energy_s(1, k)) - sqrt(energy_s(3, k));
    phi_prime = 2.0 * phi_s(1, k) - phi_s(3, k);
    r2 = sqrt(energy_s(2, k));
    phi2 = phi_s(2, k);
    temp1 = r2 * cos( phi2 ) - r_prime * cos( phi_prime );
    temp2 = r2 * sin( phi2 ) - r_prime * sin( phi_prime );
    temp3 = r2 + abs( r_prime );

    if temp3 ~= 0.0
        cw(j) = sqrt( temp1 * temp1 + temp2 * temp2 ) / temp3;
    else
        cw(j) = 0.0;
    end

    cw(j+1) = cw(j);
    cw(j+2) = cw(j);
    cw(j+3) = cw(j);
end

% Set unpredictability of the remaining spectral lines to 0.4
cw(207:HBLKSIZE) = 0.4;

% Calculate the energy and the unpredictability in the threshold
% calculated partitions
cb(1, CBANDS) = 0;
for j = 1:HBLKSIZE
    tp = partition_1(j);
    if tp > 0
        eb(tp) = eb(tp) + energy(j);
        cb(tp) = cb(tp) + cw(j)*energy(j);
    end
end
```

Program 3.2: (*Continued.*) MATLAB Code for computing unpredictability measure.

The code Section 3.4 demonstrates the calculation of spreading function given in (3.6).

The basilar excitation pattern per partition is computed by convolving the energy in each partition with the spreading function.

$$ecb(z) = \sum_{b=1}^{z_{max}} eb(z_b)spf(zm_b, zm) , \qquad (3.9)$$

```
% P 3.3 - Compute the spreading function

% s[j][i], the value of the spreading function, centered at band j, f
band i.
for i = 1:part_max
    for j = 1:part_max
        tempx = (bval_1(i) - bval_1(j))*1.05;

        % Choice of parameter a
        if j >= i
            tempx = (bval_1(i) - bval_1(j))*3;
        else
            tempx = (bval_1(i) - bval_1(j))*1.5;
        end

        % Computation of B(dz) in Eq. 3.5
        if (tempx >= 0.5) & (tempx <= 2.5)
            temp = tempx - 0.5;
            x = 8.0 * (temp*temp - 2.0 * temp);
        else
            x = 0.0;
        end
        tempx = tempx + 0.474;
        tempy = 15.811389 + 7.5*tempx - 17.5*sqrt(1.0+tempx*tempx);

        % Computation of spf in Eq. 3.7
        if tempy <= -60.0
            s3_1(i, j) = 0.0;
        else
            s3_1(i, j) = exp( (x + tempy)*LN_TO_LOG10 );
        end
    end
end
```

Program 3.3: MATLAB Code for calculating spreading function.

where zm is the mean bark value of the partition z and z_{max} is the largest partition index for a given sampling rate. Also the unpredictability measure in each partition is convolved with the spreading function to take the spreading effect into account.

$$ctb(z) = \sum_{b=1}^{z_{max}} cb(z_b)spf(zm_b, zm) .\tag{3.10}$$

Figure 3.5 illustrates the spreading functions centered at bands 4, 5, 6 and 7, respectively. Since the spreading function is applied in the perceptual domain, the spreading function is relatively uniform as a function of frequency. Figure 3.6 (a) shows the output obtained by convolving the

```
% P 3.4 - Convolve the partitioned energy and unpredictability with the
spreading function.

for b = 1:CBANDS
    ecb(b) = sum(s3_l(b, 1:CBANDS).*eb(1:CBANDS));
    ctb(b) = sum(s3_l(b, 1:CBANDS).*cb(1:CBANDS));
end
```

Program 3.4: MATLAB Code for applying spreading function.

Figure 3.5: Spreading functions centered at bands 4, 5, 6 and 7, respectively.

energy in each partition with the spreading function and the spread unpredictability is shown in Figure 3.6 (b).

3.2.4   TONALITY INDEX ESTIMATION

The masking characteristics of tonal and non-tonal components are different and hence it becomes essential to separate them [96]. The tonality index is hence computed as a function of frequency, which indicates the tonal nature of the spectral component. The tonality index in each partition is calculated based on whether the signal is predictable from the spectral lines in the two previous frames. It is computed as a linear extrapolation of the components from two prior analysis windows. Tonal components are highly predictable and hence have a relatively higher index.

To compute the tonality index, the result of the spread unpredictability measure in (3.10) is normalized using the spread signal energy in (3.9),

$$cbb(z) = \log\left(\frac{ctb(z)}{ecb(z)}\right) . \tag{3.11}$$

The expression inside the parentheses in (3.11), (ctb/ecb), is plotted in Figure 3.7 (b). It can be clearly seen that the normalization by the spread energy in each partition results in a behavior

(a)

(b)

Figure 3.6: (a) Spread energy (*ecb*), (b) Spread Unpredictability (*ctb*).

similar to the unpredictability measure in Figure 3.3 (b). Figure 3.7 (c) shows the parameter *cbb* as given in (3.11).

The measure $cbb(z)$ is then mapped onto tonality index which is a function of the partition number and whose values vary between zero and one.

$$tbb(z) = -0.299 - 0.43 * cbb(z), \quad 0 < tbb(z) < 1 . \tag{3.12}$$

Since the unpredictability measure is convolved with the spreading function that determines the masking energy at any frequency location, the resulting tonality index reflects the tonality of dominant maskers at that frequency location. The tonality indices of the threshold partitions are illustrated in Figure 3.7 (d). As described, the tonality indices range from 0 (high unpredictability) to 1 (low unpredictability) corresponding to the unpredictability. The relation between the parameters *tbb* and *cbb* given in (3.12) can also be clearly seen in the plots. As expected, tonal components have a higher tonality index compared to the non-tonal components. The code section 3.5 demonstrates the estimation of tonality index of the threshold partitions.

3.2.5   CALCULATION OF MASKING THRESHOLDS FOR THRESHOLD PARTITIONS

The masking thresholds are calculated with a higher frequency resolution than that provided by the polyphase filter bank. The masking threshold is determined by providing an offset to the excitation pattern, where the value of the offset strongly depends on the nature of the masker [97, 98]. The tonality indices evaluated for each partition are used to determine the offset of the re-normalized convolved signal energy, which converts it into the global masking level. The values for the offset are interpolated based on the tonality index of a noise masker to a frequency-dependent value defined in the standard for a tonal masker. The interpolated offset is compared with a frequency dependent

```
% P 3.5 - Calculate the tonality of each threshold calculation
partition

for b = 1:CBANDS
    if ecb(b) ~= 0.0
        cbb = ctb(b)/ecb(b);
        if cbb < 0.01
            cbb = 0.01;
        end
        cbb = log(cbb);
    else
        cbb = 0.0 ;
    end

    tbb = -0.299 - 0.43*cbb;  % conv1=-0.299, conv2=-0.43
    tbb = min(1.0, max(0.0, tbb) ) ;   % 0<tbb<1
    tonality(b) = tbb;
end
```

Program 3.5: MATLAB Code for estimating tonality index.

minimum value, *minval*, defined in the standard and the larger value is used as the signal to noise ratio (SNR). In the MPEG-1 standard, Noise masking Tone (NMT) is set to 6 dB and Tone masking Noise (TMN) to 29 dB for all partitions. The offset is obtained by weighting the maskers with the estimated tonality index.

$$O(z) = 29tbb(z) + 6(1 - tbb(z)) . \qquad (3.13)$$

The SNR in each of the threshold partitions can be computed as,

$$SNR(z) = \max[\min val(z), O(z)] , \qquad (3.14)$$

where $\min val(z)$ is the lower limit for SNR in the partition. It is predetermined and stored in tables for the corresponding sampling rates. The computed SNR for each threshold partition is shown in Figure 3.8 (a). Transforming SNR into the power domain yields,

$$bc(z) = 10^{\frac{-SNR(z)}{10}} . \qquad (3.15)$$

The spreading function, because of its shape, increases the energy estimates in each band due to the effects of spreading. Hence, a renormalization process is used, by multiplying each partition by inverse of the energy gain, assuming a uniform energy of 1 in the partition.

$$enb(z) = ecb(z)rnorm(z) , \qquad (3.16)$$

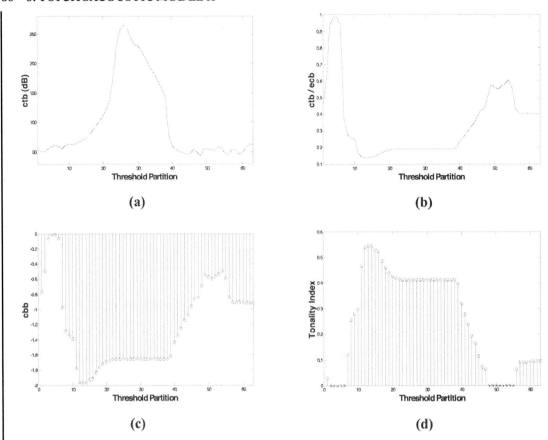

Figure 3.7: (a) Spread unpredictability (ctb), (b) Plot of ctb/ecb, (c) Normalized spread unpredictability (cbb), (d) Tonality index (tbb).

where

$$rnorm(z) = \frac{1}{\sum\limits_{b=0}^{z_{max}} spf(zm_b, zm)} \; . \tag{3.17}$$

The actual energy threshold for each partition is hence given by

$$nb(z) = enb(z)bc(z) \; . \tag{3.18}$$

Figure 3.8 (b) illustrates the energy, spread energy and the actual threshold energy in each threshold calculation partition.

```
% P 3.6 - Calculate the energy threshold for each partition
for b = 1:CBANDS
   % Calculation of SNR for each partition
   % TMN=29.0,NMT=6.0 for all calculation partitions
     SNR_l(b) = max( minval(b), 29.0*tbb+6.0*(1.0-tbb) );
end

% calculate the threshold for each partition
nb(1:CBANDS)=ecb(1:CBANDS).*norm_l(1:CBANDS).*exp(-...
SNR_l(1:CBANDS)*LN_TO_LOG10);
```

Program 3.6: MATLAB Code for calculating energy threshold.

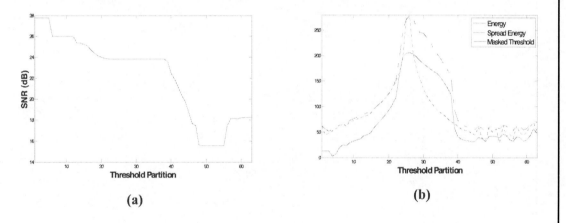

(a)

(b)

Figure 3.8: (a) SNR of the threshold partitions, (b) Masked thresholds of the threshold partitions.

The threshold derived for the current frame is compared with that of the two previous frames and the threshold in quiet. The maximum of the three values is chosen to be the actual threshold.

$$thr(z) = \max \left[Tq(z), \min \left[nb(z), nb_{t-1}(z), nb_{t-2}(z) \right] \right], \tag{3.19}$$

$$nb_{j-1}(z) = 2.nb(z), \tag{3.20}$$

$$nb_{j-2}(z) = 16.nb(z), \tag{3.21}$$

where $Tq(f)$ is the absolute threshold of hearing, $nb_{j-1}(z)$ and $nb_{j-2}(z)$ are the energy thresholds from the two previous frames. The absolute threshold of hearing (threshold in quiet) characterizes the amount of energy needed in a pure tone such that it can be detected by a listener in a noiseless environment [99]. The threshold is well approximated by the nonlinear function [100],

$$Tq(f) = 3.64 \left(\frac{f}{1000} \right)^{-0.8} - 6.5e^{-0.6\left(\frac{f}{1000}-3.3 \right)^2} + 10^{-3} \left(\frac{f}{1000} \right)^4 \text{ (dB SPL)}, \tag{3.22}$$

which is representative of a young listener with acute hearing. Figure 3.9 illustrates the threshold in quiet curve as a function of frequency. The threshold in quiet is set to be the lower bound on the audibility of sound and can be interpreted as a maximum allowable energy level for coding distortions introduced in the frequency domain. The absolute threshold is typically expressed in terms of Sound Pressure Level (SPL) [88]. The SPL gives the intensity of the sound pressure in decibels relative to an internationally defined reference level.

$$L_{SPL}(\text{dB}) = 20 \log_{10}(p/p_0) , \qquad (3.23)$$

where p is the sound pressure of the stimulus in Pascals and p_0 is the standard reference level of $20\mu Pa$.

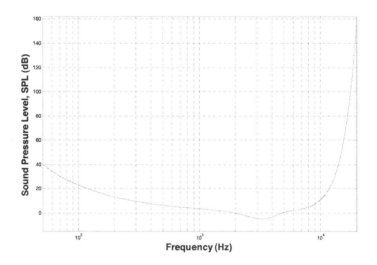

Figure 3.9: Approximate spectral curve for the threshold in quiet.

3.2.6   PRE-ECHO DETECTION AND WINDOW SWITCHING

Pre-echoes occur when a signal with a sharp attack begins near the end of a transform block immediately following a region of low energy [73]. This situation can arise when encoding recordings of percussive instruments such as the triangle, the glockenspiel, or the castanets, for example shown in Figure 3.10 (a). For a block-based algorithm, when quantization and encoding are performed, the time-frequency uncertainty dictates that the inverse transform will spread quantization distortion evenly in time throughout the reconstructed block [Figure 3.10 (b)]. This results in unmasked distortion throughout the low-energy region preceding in time the signal attack at the decoder. The MPEG-1 algorithm uses the MDCT to transform the blocks containing the subband data, which in turn are encoded and transmitted. The longer the block length the better is the frequency

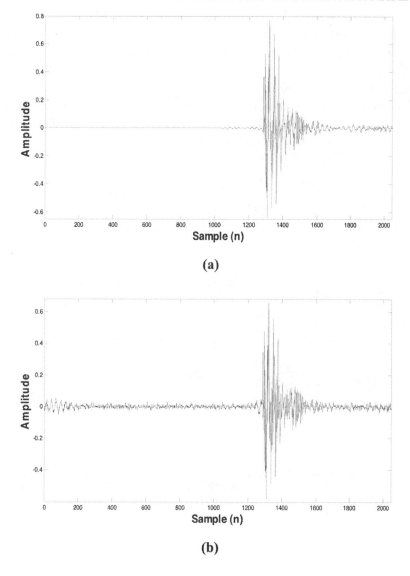

(a)

(b)

Figure 3.10: Pre-echo example: (a) uncoded castanets, (b) transform coded castanets.

resolution, which comes at the expense of losing time resolution. For quasi-stationary signals, longer blocks provide better compression. On the other hand, the transients are well captured by shorter blocks. Hence, adapting the size of blocks based on the statistics of the signal will yield best results. When long windows are used for sharper transients, the signal is coarsely quantized. In the time domain, the quantization noise spreads over the entire block and it would create a perceptible noise at the beginning of the audio. Pre-echo can be controlled by detecting such transients and making a decision to switch to short windows [101, 102]. It is implemented by calculating the perceptual entropy from the masking threshold and switching the window when it exceeds a pre-determined value [86].

Perceptual entropy indicates the average minimum number of bits per frequency sample needed to encode a signal without introducing a perceptual difference with respect to the original signal. It gives a lower bound estimate for the perceptual coding based on the computed mask threshold. Perceptual Entropy can be defined as,

$$PE = -\sum_{b=1}^{Z_{max}} \left[cbwidth(b).\log\left(\frac{thr(b)}{eb(b)+1}\right)\right], \qquad (3.24)$$

where $cbwidth(b)$ is the width of the calculated threshold partition and $eb(b)$ is the energy in the threshold partition.

```
% P 3.7 - Pre-echo detection and calculation of Perceptual Entropy
window switching

% pre-echo control
for b = 1:CBANDS
    temp_1 = min(nb(b), min(2.0*nb_1(chn, b),16.0*nb_2(chn, b)));
    thr(b) = max(qthr_1(b), temp_1);
    nb_2(chn, b) = nb_1(chn, b);
    nb_1(chn, b) = nb(b);
end

% calculate perceptual entropy
pe(gr, chn) = 0.0;
for b = 1:CBANDS
    tp = min(0.0, log((thr(b)+1.0)/(eb(b)+1.0)) );
    pe(gr, chn) = pe(gr, chn) - numlines(b) * tp ;
end
```

Program 3.7: MATLAB Code for pre-echo detection and calculation of PE.

An empirically predetermined value is used based on which window switching decision is made. The state-machine for the window switching is shown in Figure 3.11. It can be observed that whenever a sharp attack is identified or the Perceptual Entropy exceeds the predetermined value (1800), the algorithm switches to a *short* window. Notice that there are two transition windows, *start* and *stop*, which are used between the *long* and *short* windows. A description of the different window types and the scheme of window-switching can be found in Chapter 4. The corresponding program is listed in Program 3.8.

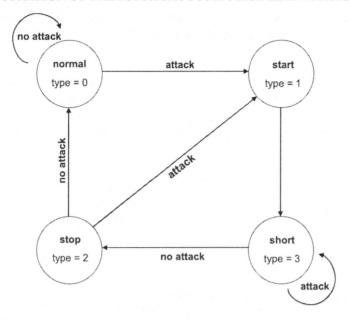

Figure 3.11: Window switching state machine.

3.2.7   ESTIMATION OF SMR

In MP3 encoding, the threshold is not spread over the FFT lines as done in the case of psychoacoustic model I. Instead, the threshold calculation partitions are converted directly into scalefactor bands. In general, scalefactors are employed to determine the quantization step size for a particular band to ensure that the resulting quantization noise level falls below the computed masked threshold. Scalefactor bands are groups of frequency lines which are scaled by a single scalefactor and they approximate critical bands. Hence, the signal to mask (SMR) ratio is evaluated in the scalefactor bands. There are predetermined tables which indicate the mapping between threshold partitions and the scalefactor band. For each sampling rate, there are 21 bands for long windows and 12 bands for short windows.

The energy in each scalefactor band is given by

$$en(sb) = w1.eb(bu) + \sum_{b=bu+1}^{b=b0-1} eb(b) + w2.eb(b0) \, , \qquad (3.25)$$

where $b0$ and bu are parameters used for converting threshold partitions into scale-factor bands. The threshold in each scalefactor band is given by

$$thm(sb) = w1.thr(bu) + \sum_{b=bu+1}^{b=b0-1} thr(b) + w2.thr(b0) . \qquad (3.26)$$

The final output of the psychoacoustic model II, the signal-to-mask ratio (SMR) in each scale-factor band is defined as

$$SMR(sb) = \frac{thm(sb)}{en(sb)} . \qquad (3.27)$$

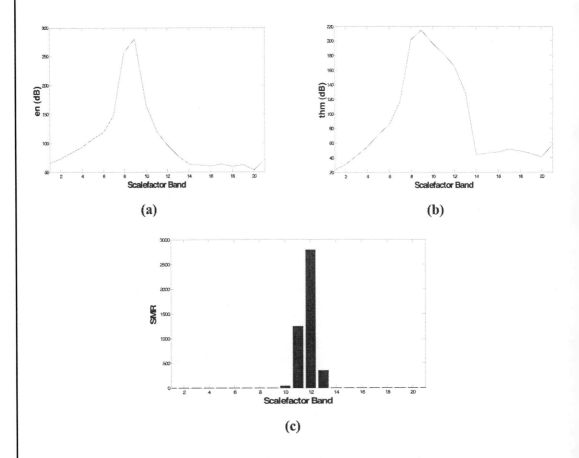

(a)

(b)

(c)

Figure 3.12: (a) Energy in scalefactor bands, (b) Thresholds in scalefactor bands, (c) Signal-to-mask ratio in scalefactor bands.

Figure 3.12 (c) illustrates the SMR in the scalefactor bands for the case when a long window is used. The program listing Program 3.8 shows the window switching and threshold computation for the case when long blocks are used. Similar steps can be carried out to perform the window switching and threshold computation for the case when short windows are to be used. Thus, the threshold calculation partitions are converted to codec partitions (scale-factor bands) and the SMR values computed are forwarded to the bit/noise allocation algorithm.

```
% P 3.8 - Window Switching State Machine and Calculation of SMR

switch_pe = 1800;
blocktype = NORM_TYPE;

if pe(gr, chn) < switch_pe          % no attack : use long blocks
    switch blocktype_old(chn)
    case NORM_TYPE,
    case STOP_TYPE,
        blocktype = NORM_TYPE;
    case SHORT_TYPE,
        blocktype = STOP_TYPE;
    case START_TYPE,
        error(disp(sprintf('Error in block selecting\n')));
    end

    % threshold calculation (part 2)
    % Calculation of energy and threshold in each scale-factor band
    for sb = 1:SBMAX_1
        en(sb) = w1_1(sb) * eb(bu_1(sb)+1) + w2_1(sb) * eb(bo_1(sb)+1);
        thm(sb) = w1_1(sb) *thr(bu_1(sb)+1) + w2_1(sb) * thr(bo_1(sb)+1);

        b = bu_1(sb)+1:bo_1(sb);
        en(sb) = en(sb) + sum(eb(b));
        thm(sb) = thm(sb) + sum(thr(b));

        if en(sb) ~= 0.0
            ratio(chn, sb) = thm(sb)/en(sb);
          else
            ratio(chn, sb) = 0.0;
        end
    end
end
```

Program 3.8: MATLAB Code for window switching and calculation of SMR.

3.3   SUMMARY

This chapter presented a detailed description of the psychoacoustic model II and its use in the analysis of masking characteristics of audio signals. The MPEG-1 Layer-3 algorithm achieves compression by allowing the quantization noise in the frequency subbands where the human ear is the least sensitive. The psychoacoustic model determines the maximum noise level which would be just perceptible (masking level) in each of the subbands from the input audio. Since quantization noise is directly related to the number of bits used by the quantizer, the bit allocation algorithm determines the bit assignment such that the audible distortion is minimized. The psychoacoustic model II does not make a dichotomous distinction between tonal and non-tonal components. Instead, it transforms the spectral data to a partition domain and estimates the tonality index in each partition. This measure actually determines the amount of masking. The partition domain approximates the critical band ranges. The reader in need of further details on psychoacoustics principles and the model used in perceptual coders is directed to [27, 72, 86, 88, 94].

CHAPTER 4

MDCT

4.1 DESCRIPTION

To achieve maximum coding gain, signals with strong and fine harmonic content require a high frequency resolution and coarse time resolution because the masking thresholds need to be localized in frequency. On the other hand, fast transients need adequate time resolution (short windows) to accurately estimate highly time localized temporal masking thresholds. However, most audio signals are highly non-stationary in nature and contain both steady-state and transient intervals. As a result, an effective coder should make adaptive decisions regarding the optimal time-frequency decomposition. This implies that the filter bank will have time-varying temporal and frequency resolutions. This motivates the use of hybrid filter structures in which switching decisions are made based on the changing signal characteristics. For this reason, the outputs of the 32-band polyphase filterbank are processed using the modified discrete cosine transform (MDCT) block. In essence, the 32 subband samples are further subdivided in the frequency domain using MDCT, thereby providing a good frequency resolution. The polyphase filter bank and the MDCT are together referred as the *hybrid filterbank*.

Being a lapped transform, the MDCT avoids artifacts from the block boundaries, in addition to providing energy compaction. The other important reason for the widespread use of MDCT in certain coding standards is the availability of FFT-based algorithms, which makes it suitable for real-time applications [103, 104]. The window switching for MDCT is controlled using the perceptual entropy measure obtained from the psychoacoustic module. After the audio signal is transformed to the frequency domain using the MDCT, a partial cancellation of the aliasing introduced in the analysis filter bank is performed. Figure 4.1 illustrates the hybrid filterbank structure used in MPEG-1 Layer III algorithm.

4.2 ILLUSTRATION OF THE MDCT WITH MATLAB CODE

4.2.1 MDCT CALCULATION

MDCT is a lapped transform that has half as many outputs as inputs. It is based on the type-IV discrete cosine transform with 50% overlap between the adjacent time windows. Thus, the MDCT basis functions extend across two blocks in time, thereby eliminating the block artifacts. Despite the 50% overlap, the MDCT is critically sampled and only M samples are generated for every $2M$ samples of the input block. Hence, it produces 18 frequency components for 36 time domain samples. The MDCT basis functions have a length $N = 2M$, where M denotes the number of subbands.

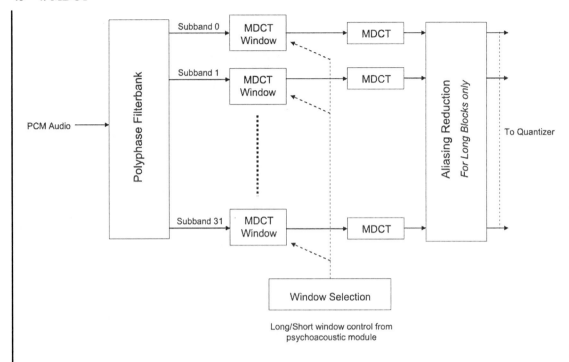

Figure 4.1: Illustration of the hybrid filter bank.

Given the analysis window $h(n)$, the output of the MDCT can be defined as

$$X(k) = \sqrt{\frac{2}{M}} \sum_{n=0}^{N-1} x(n)h(n) \cos\left[\left(n + \frac{M+1}{2}\right)\left(k + \frac{1}{2}\right)\frac{\pi}{M}\right],$$

$$\text{where, } k = 0, 1, ..., N/2 - 1 .$$

(4.1)

   The analysis window $h(n)$ is chosen based on the perceptual entropy (PE) measure obtained from the psychoacoustic module. In effect, the MPEG codec changes the window length to match the signal characteristics of the input. A long window is used to maximize coding gain and achieve good channel separation for stationary segments. Short windows are used to localize time domain artifacts when pre-echos are likely. Because of the time overlap between the basis vectors, boundary filters or transition windows are used.

   Clearly, the forward MDCT in (4.1) performs a series of inner products between the analysis filter impulse responses and the input. Prior to applying the MDCT to the subbands, each of the odd samples of odd subbands must undergo a frequency inversion correction so that the spectral lines appear in a proper ascending order. As seen in Program 4.1, the inversion is applied by multiplying each odd sample by -1 to compensate for the frequency inversion of the polyphase filter bank.

```
% P 4.1 - Frequency Inversion Correction

for gr = 1:mode_gr % Granules
    for ch = 1:chn % Channels

        cod_info = get_gr_info_from_l3_side(l3_side, gr, ch);
        % Type of the window as obtained from the side information
        block_type = cod_info.block_type;
        mixed_block_flag = cod_info.mixed_block_flag;

        % Compensate for inversion in the analysis filter bank
        % Inversion is applied only to the odd time samples of the odd
          subbands
        band = 2:2:32; time_index = 2:2:18;
        S(ch, gr, band, time_index) = -S(ch, gr, band, time_index);
```

Program 4.1: MATLAB Code for frequency inversion correction.

The psychoacoustic model detects the pre-echo condition and chooses short windows for better time resolution and long windows for improved frequency resolution. When the perceptual entropy measure exceeds 1800, the MDCT filterbank is switched to use short windows. To maintain perfect reconstruction of MDCT, short and long windows are not switched instantaneously. For this purpose, two transition windows, start and stop are provided. The windows used in MDCT window switching are illustrated in Figure 4.2. It can be observed that the size of a short block is 12 samples, whereas that of a long block is 36 samples. In the short block mode, three short blocks with 50% overlap are used. Switching from a long to short window includes a transition start window while a stop window is placed in the transition from a short to a long window. Each block of data processed by MDCT contains 36 samples.

Figure 4.3 illustrates a typical case of window switching. It graphically depicts the switching from a long window to short window and back. There is a sequence of three short windows between the two long windows, with transition windows in between. For the first granule, the block of data passed to the MDCT is built using 18 samples of current subband and 18 samples from the memory. The memory contains 18 samples of second granule of the same subband in the previous frame. For the second granule, the block is built using 18 current samples and 18 samples from the first granule of the same subband in the current frame. Program 4.2 illustrates the above procedure for building data vector from the subbands for MDCT.

The calculation of the analysis window coefficients for the different windows as shown in Figure 4.2 can be found in the file *mdct_h.m*. Program 4.3 shows the calculation of coefficients for the different types of windows.

For a particular block of data, all the filterbank channels can have the same MDCT analysis window (short or long) or a mixed mode in which the two lowest frequency subbands have long

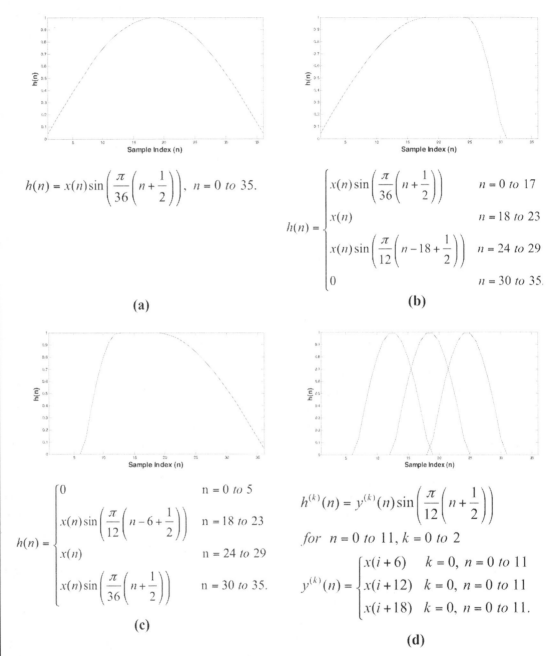

$$h(n) = x(n)\sin\left(\frac{\pi}{36}\left(n+\frac{1}{2}\right)\right), \quad n = 0 \ to \ 35.$$

(a)

$$h(n) = \begin{cases} x(n)\sin\left(\dfrac{\pi}{36}\left(n+\dfrac{1}{2}\right)\right) & n = 0 \ to \ 17 \\[2mm] x(n) & n = 18 \ to \ 23 \\[2mm] x(n)\sin\left(\dfrac{\pi}{12}\left(n-18+\dfrac{1}{2}\right)\right) & n = 24 \ to \ 29 \\[2mm] 0 & n = 30 \ to \ 35. \end{cases}$$

(b)

$$h(n) = \begin{cases} 0 & n = 0 \ to \ 5 \\[2mm] x(n)\sin\left(\dfrac{\pi}{12}\left(n-6+\dfrac{1}{2}\right)\right) & n = 18 \ to \ 23 \\[2mm] x(n) & n = 24 \ to \ 29 \\[2mm] x(n)\sin\left(\dfrac{\pi}{36}\left(n+\dfrac{1}{2}\right)\right) & n = 30 \ to \ 35. \end{cases}$$

(c)

$$h^{(k)}(n) = y^{(k)}(n)\sin\left(\frac{\pi}{12}\left(n+\frac{1}{2}\right)\right)$$

$$for \ \ n = 0 \ to \ 11, k = 0 \ to \ 2$$

$$y^{(k)}(n) = \begin{cases} x(i+6) & k = 0, \ n = 0 \ to \ 11 \\ x(i+12) & k = 0, \ n = 0 \ to \ 11 \\ x(i+18) & k = 0, \ n = 0 \ to \ 11. \end{cases}$$

(d)

Figure 4.2: Illustration of the windows used in the MDCT filter bank: (a) long window, (b) start window, (c) stop window, (d) 3 short windows.

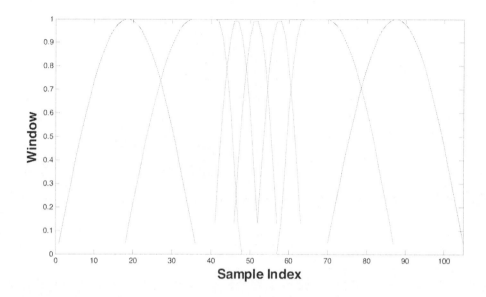

Figure 4.3: Illustration of a typical window switching.

blocks while the remaining 30 bands have short blocks. This ensures better frequency resolution at lower frequencies while having a higher time resolution for higher frequencies. The MDCT coefficients are computed as defined in Equation (4.1) and illustrated in Program 4.4.

4.2.2 ALIAS REDUCTION

The aliasing introduced due to the downsampling in the polyphase filter bank can be partially reduced at this stage, once MDCT maps the subband samples into the frequency domain. The alias reduction is applied only to the long blocks. The anti-aliasing butterfly for the encoder is shown in Figure 4.4. Each anti-aliasing butterfly is an orthonormal transformation applied to one of the eight designated pairs of spectral lines. They do not affect the reconstruction properties of the filterbank, but improve the compression factor of the coder by trying to contain the energy within each subband. The alias reduction computation can described as

$$rMDCT\,(18sb - i - 1) = rMDCT\,(18sb - i - 1)\,cs\,(i) - rMDCT\,(18sb + i)\,ca\,(i)\,,$$
$$rMDCT\,(18sb + i) = rMDCT\,(18sb + i)\,cs\,(i) - rMDCT\,(18sb - i - 1)\,ca\,(i)\,,\quad (4.2)$$

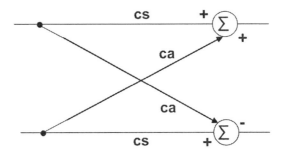

Figure 4.4: Alias reduction butterfly for the encoder.

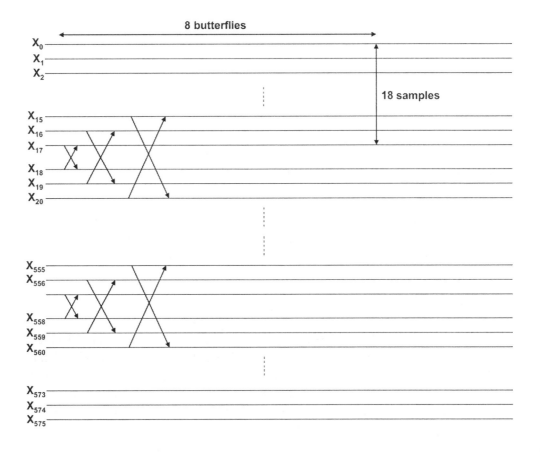

Figure 4.5: Alias reduction operations for a granule of MDCT data.

```
% P 4.2 - Build data from the subbands for MDCT computation

% MDCT of subband data using 18 previous subband samples + 18 current
subband samples

for band = 0:31
% For the first granule, get 18 previous subband samples from memory
  if gr == 1
     MDCTtime_in(1:18) = MDCTmemory(ch, band+1, 1:18);
     MDCTtime_in(19:36) = S(ch, gr, band+1, 1:18);
% For the second granule, get 18 previous subband samples from the
first granule
  else % gr == 2
     MDCTtime_in(1:18) = S(ch, gr-1, band+1, 1:18);
     MDCTtime_in(19:36) = S(ch, gr, band+1, 1:18);
  End
```

Program 4.2: MATLAB Code for building input data vector for the MDCT.

where $i = 0$ to 7 and $sb = 1$ to 31. Here, the indices of the array $rMDCT$ label the frequency lines in a granule, arranged in the lowest frequency to the highest frequency, with zero being the index of the lowest frequency line and 575 being the index of the highest. The butterfly coefficients cs and ci are calculated as

$$cs_i = \frac{1}{\sqrt{1 + c_i^2}} \quad \text{and} \quad ca_i = \frac{cs_i}{\sqrt{1 + c_i^2}}, \tag{4.3}$$

where c_i indicate the Layer III coefficients for alias reduction [27].

Figure 4.5 illustrates the alias reduction operations for a granule (576 samples) of MDCT data. Unlike the usual time-frequency plane, they are now rearranged for alias reduction, first in the order of subband and then in time. Therefore, 18 time-domain samples of each subband are grouped together. The MATLAB implementation of this alias-reduction procedure can found in Program 4.5.

4.3 SUMMARY

In Chapter 4, we outlined the design of a hybrid filterbank structure, in which switching decisions are made based on the changing signal characteristics. The MPEG-1 Layer III algorithm uses a set of 512-tap FIR filters for both analysis and synthesis of the PCM audio data. These alias-cancellation filters are designed such that high sidelobe attenuation is achieved. This algorithm employs an efficient implementation of these filters using a polyphase structure thereby reducing the computations. In the Layer-3 algorithm, each of the 32 subbands from the analysis subband filter bank is further subdivided divided into 18 spectral lines using the MDCT followed by the

```
% P 4.3 - Generation of Analysis Window coefficients

% type 0: normal = long blocks
win(1, 1:36) = sin(pi/36*((0:35) + 0.5));

% type 1: start block
win(2, 1:18) = sin(pi/36*((0:17) + 0.5));
win(2, 19:24) = 1;
k = 24:29;
win(2, 25:30) = sin(pi/12*(k + 0.5 - 18));
clear k;

% type 3: stop block
k = 6:11;
win(4, 7:12) = sin(pi/12*(k + 0.5 - 6));
clear k;
win(4, 13:18) = 1;
win(4, 19:36) = sin(pi/36*((18:35) + 0.5));

% type 2: short block
win(3, 1:12) = sin(pi/12*((0:11) + 0.5));
```

Program 4.3: MATLAB Code for computing analysis window coefficients.

application of alias reduction butterflies. The MDCT module provides better frequency resolution and the transient effects are controlled using different window functions. The reader in need of further details on pseudo QMF and its design is referred to [105, 106, 107, 108, 109, 110, 111].

```
% P 4.4 - The core MDCT routine

% INPUT VARIABLES
%    Time_in: vector of 36 time-domain subband outputs
%    blk_type: type of time-freq block - long, short, transition
% OUTPUT VARIABLES
%    Freq_out: vector of 18 MDCT-domain subband outputs

function [Freq_out] = MDCTcore(Time_in, blk_type)

% Initialized by mdct_h.m
global win cos_s cos_l;
Freq_out = zeros(1, 18);

% type 2: short block, but indexing for win[] = win(3, :)
if blk_type == 2
   N = 12; k = 1:N;
   for l = 0:2
      for m = 0:N/2-1
         Freq_out(3*m+l+1) = sum(win(blk_type+1,
                               k).*Time_in(6+6*l+k).*cos_s(m+1, k));
      end
   end
else
   N = 36; k = 1:N;
   for m = 1:N/2
      Freq_out(m) = sum(win(blk_type+1, k).*Time_in(k).*cos_l(m, k));
   end
end
return
```

Program 4.4: MATLAB Code for computing MDCT coefficients.

```matlab
% P 4.5 -  Alias reduction butterflies for long blocks

if ( block_type ~= 2 )
% flash the alias-reduction block
  updateMainGui('Alias Reduction', 'start');

for band = 1:31 %Index for subband
 for k = 0:7 % Index for the spectral line

  bu = rMDCT(gr, ch, band*18-k)*cs(k+1) + rMDCT(gr, ch,
            band*18+k+1)*ca(k+1);

  bd = rMDCT(gr, ch, band*18+k+1)*cs(k+1) - rMDCT(gr, ch, band*18-
            k)*ca(k+1);

  rMDCT(gr, ch, band*18-k) = bu;
  rMDCT(gr, ch, band*18+k+1) = bd;
 end
end
```

Program 4.5: MATLAB Code for alias-reduction of MDCT data.

CHAPTER 5

Bit Allocation, Quantization and Coding

5.1 DESCRIPTION

The bit allocation process determines the number of bits allocated to each of the subbands based on the information obtained from the psychoacoustic module. The Layer III loop module performs the key steps of non-uniform quantization and Huffman coding of the frequency lines from the MDCT module. Bit allocation and quantization of the spectral lines are realized in a nested loop procedure. The inner loop adjusts the non-uniform quantizer step sizes for each block until the number of bits required to encode the transform components falls within the available bit budget. The outer loop evaluates the quality of the encoded signal (analysis-by-synthesis) in terms of quantization noise relative to the masked thresholds. The non-uniform quantization depends on the variation of the audio signal and does not have a fixed execution time.

In Figure 5.1, we consider the case of a single masking tone occurring at the center of a critical band. Audio intensity levels in the figure are given in terms of Sound Pressure Level (dB). In the illustration, a hypothetical masking tone occurs at some masking level. This generates an excitation along the basilar membrane that is modeled by a spreading function and a corresponding masking threshold. For the band under consideration, the minimum masking threshold denotes the in-band minimum of the spreading function. Assuming the masker is quantized using an m-bit uniform scalar quantizer, noise might be introduced at the level m. SMR and noise-to-mask ratio (NMR) denote the log distances from the minimum masking threshold to the masker and noise levels, respectively. The Layer III encoder quantizes the spectral values by allocating the appropriate number of bits needed in each subband to maintain perceptual transparency at a given bit-rate. It controls and shapes the spectrum of the quantization noise to lie below audible levels. Therefore, the scheme is referred to as noise allocation, as opposed to bit allocation.

The bit allocation process of the Layer III encoder illustrated in Figure 5.2 can be described in three levels [27]. The top level, *loops frame program*, determines the scalefactor selection information (*scfsi*). The unit referred as the *outer loop* calculates the allowed distortion for each scalefactor band, as determined by the psychoacoustic module. It also computes the maximum number of bits available for each granule based on the bit reservoir size and the perceptual entropy. The *inner loop* quantizes the input vectors and modifies the quantizer step size until the output vector can be encoded with the available number of bits. The *outer loop* checks the distortion introduced by quantization in each scale factor band and if it exceeds the allowed distortion, amplifies the scalefactor band and calls

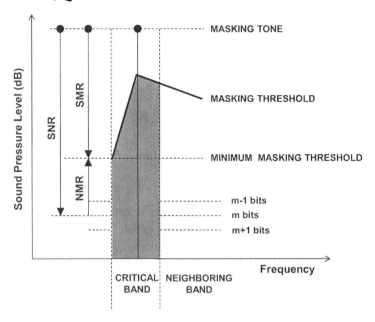

Figure 5.1: Illustration of simultaneous masking ([73, 93]).

the *inner loop* again. The encoder thus varies the quantizers iteratively using the inner and the outer loops to perform bit allocation.

The quantized values are encoded using Huffman coding. Huffman coding is a lossless entropy encoding algorithm and uses variable-length code tables. Noise shaping is performed to limit the quantization noise below the masking threshold. Hence, a global gain value that determines the quantization step size, and scalefactors that determine the noise shaping factors for each scalefactor band, are applied before the actual quantization. The process of finding the optimal gain and scalefactors for a given block at a specified bit-rate, using the Just Noticeable Difference (JND) thresholds obtained from the psychoacoustic module, is performed in the Layer III loop module.

5.2   THE LOOPS FRAME FUNCTION

5.2.1   CALCULATION OF THE SCALEFACTOR SELECTION INFORMATION (SCFSI)

The *scfsi* determines if the scalefactors of the first granule can be re-used for the second granule in the coding process. This implies that these scalefactors need not be transmitted twice and hence the bits saved in this process can be used in the Huffman coding. If the encoder operates in short block mode, then different scalefactors are always transmitted for each granule. The parameter *scfsi*

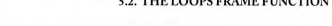

Figure 5.2: Implementation of the Layer III loop module.

in Layer III is represented by one bit for each subband. To evaluate the parameter *scfsi*, the following information is needed for each granule.

- The block type (long/short).

- The total energy in the granule

$$en\_tot = int \left\{ \log_2 \left(\sum_{i=1}^{n} |xr(i)|^2 \right) \right\} , \qquad (5.1)$$

where n is the total number of spectral values and xr indicates the unquantized MDCT components.

- The energy in each scalefactor band, i.e.,

$$en(sb) = int \left\{ \log_2 \left(\sum_{i=lbl(sb)}^{lbl(sb)+bw(sb)-1} |xr(i)|^2 \right) \right\} , \qquad (5.2)$$

where $lbl(sb)$ refers to the index of the first coefficient belonging to the scalefactor band sb and $bw(sb)$ indicates the number of coefficients within the scalefactor band.

- The distortion allowed for each scalefactor band, which is given by

$$xm(sb) = int \left\{ \log_2 (x\min(i)) \right\} , \qquad (5.3)$$

where $xmin(sb)$ is the allowed distortion for each scalefactor band obtained from the psychoacoustics module.

The scalefactors for the first granule are always transmitted. When the second granule is encoded, the following comparisons of the two granules are performed in order to determine if the parameter $scfsi$ can be enabled.

- All spectral values are not zero,

- The granules do not contain short blocks,

- $|en\_tot_0 - en\_tot_1| < en\_tot_{krit}$,

- $\sum_{\text{all scalefactor bands}} |en(sb)_0 - en(sb)_1| < en\_dif_{krit}$.

The constants with the subscript *krit* have been pre-determined such that $scfsi$ is enabled only if there is similarity in energy/distortion. If either of these criteria is not satisfied, $scfsi$ is disabled, i.e., it is set to 0 in all scalefactor bands. Here, index 0 indicates the first granule and index 1 refers to the second.

5.3 DISTORTION CONTROL (OUTER LOOP)

The outer iteration loop controls the noise produced by the quantization of the frequency lines which is performed in the inner iteration loop. The scalefactors are used to shape the quantization noise. Quantization noise can be spectrally shaped such that it can be masked completely. The spectral shaping of the noise is done by multiplying the lines within the scalefactor bands with the actual scalefactors before quantization. In Layer III, several frequency lines are grouped to form scalefactor bands that are designed to resemble critical bands as closely as possible. The division of the spectrum into scalefactor bands is fixed for every block length and sampling frequency and is stored at both the encoder and decoder. The scalefactors are logarithmically quantized and the quantization step size is set by the parameter *scalefac_scale*. The scalefactor for frequency lines, beyond the highest line indicated by the tables, is zero, which means that the actual multiplication factor is 1. The distortion control loop always begins with *scalefac_scale=0*. If the distortion in any of the scalefactor bands exceeds the permissible distortion, the quantization step size is suitably adjusted for those scalefactor bands. Figure 5.3 shows the block diagram describing the implementation of the outer loop.

The scalefactors of all the scalefactor bands, *scalefac_l* and *scalefac_s*, and the quantizer step size are saved in this loop. If the execution of the outer loop is terminated, without having reached the final result, these values together with the quantized spectrum can be transmitted. For each outer iteration loop, the inner iteration loop is called to perform the actual quantization. The parameters required for performing rate control (inner loop) are the outputs of the hybrid filterbank with the scalefactors applied to the lines within the corresponding scalefactor bands and the total number of available bits. The actual distortion introduced by the quantization in the inner loop for each of the scalefactor bands is calculated as

$$xfsf(sb) = \sum_{i=lbl(sb)}^{lbl(sb)+bw(sb)-1} \frac{\left(|xr(i)| - ix(i)^4/3 * \sqrt[4]{2}^{qquant+quantaf} \right)^2}{bandwidth(sb)} , \qquad (5.4)$$

where $lbl(sb)$ indicates the index of the coefficient representing the lowest frequency in a scalefactor band, $bw(sb)$ is the number of coefficients in the band and $qquant$ indicates the quantizer step size.

The option for preemphasis, determined by the parameter *preflag*, enables the outer loop to amplify the upper part of the spectrum using the preemphasis tables. The *preflag* is switched *on* if the actual distortion exceeds the threshold in all of the four upper scalefactor bands, after the first call of the inner iteration loop. Furthermore, all spectral values of the scalefactor bands which have a distortion that exceeds the allowed distortion need to be amplified by a factor, which is transmitted by the parameter *scalefac_scale*. The process of the outer loop is continued until

- There is no scalefactor band that exceeds the allowed distortion;

- All scalefactor bands are already amplified;

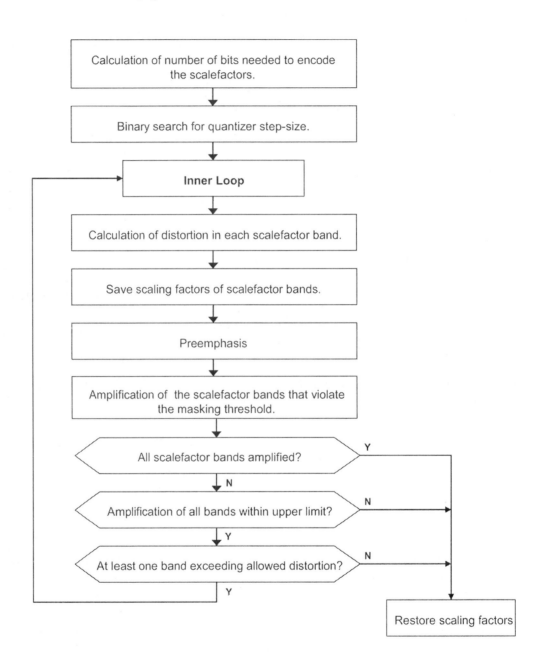

Figure 5.3: Implementation of the Outer Loop (Distortion Control).

- Amplification of at least one band exceeds the upper limit, which is determined by the transmission format of the scalefactors;

- Time-out is reached, in case of real-time implementations.

It can be seen from the code section in Program 5.1 that the two variables, *status* and over, control the execution of the outer loop. The parameter *status* is zero if there is at least a scalefactor band that has not been amplified and this indicates that the outer loop should be executed again. The variable *over* indicates if there is at least one scalefactor band that violates the masking threshold. Figure 5.4 illustrates two cases that demonstrate the effect of the two parameters in the outer loop execution. In Figure 5.4 (a) the termination is caused by the variable *status*, whereas in Figure 5.4 (b) the variable *over* terminates the outer loop.

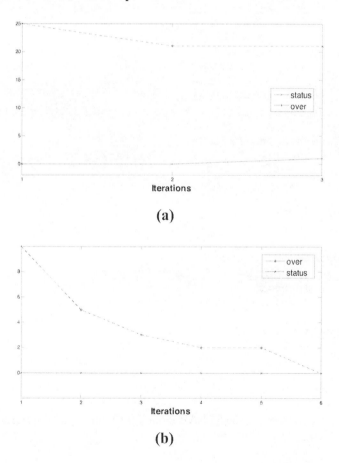

(a)

(b)

Figure 5.4: Illustration of the effect of the variables *status* and *over* in the outer loop execution.

```
% P 5.1 - Outer Iteration Loop

status = 0;
over = 2^32;      % actual value returned by amp_scalefac_bands()

while status == 0 & over > 0
   cod_info = get_gr_info_from_l3_side(l3_side, gr, ch);
   iteration = iteration + 1;
   cod_info.part2_length = part2_length(fr_ps, gr, ch, l3_side);
   huff_bits = max_bits - cod_info.part2_length;

   % Call Inner Loop
   [bits xr_quant cod_info] = inner_loop( xr, huff_bits, cod_info);

   % Distortion Calculation
   xfsf = calc_noise(xr, xr_quant, cod_info, xfsf);

   % Save scaling factors
   scalesave_l(1:CBLIMIT) = scalefac.l(gr, ch, 1:CBLIMIT);
   for sfb = 1:SFB_SMAX
      scalesave_s(sfb, 1:3) = scalefac.s(gr, ch, sfb, 1:3);
   end
   save_preflag  = cod_info.preflag;
   save_compress = cod_info.scalefac_compress;

   % Update the struct
   l3_side = put_gr_info_to_l3_side(cod_info, l3_side, gr, ch);
   % Preemphasis
   [xr, l3_xmin, l3_side] = preemphasis(xr, xfsf, l3_xmin, gr, ch,
                                        l3_side);
   % Amplify scalefactor bands
   [over xr l3_xmin scalefac] = amp_scalefac_bands(xr, xfsf, l3_xmin
                                   l3_side, scalefac, gr, ch, iterati

   cod_info = get_gr_info_from_l3_side(l3_side, gr, ch);
```

Program 5.1: MATLAB Code for Outer loop. (*Continues.*)

```
% Checking for Termination
   status = loop_break(scalefac, cod_info, gr, ch);

   if status == 0
       [status cod_info] = scale_bitcount(scalefac, cod_info, gr, ch);
       % Update the struct
       l3_side = put_gr_info_to_l3_side(cod_info, l3_side, gr, ch);
   end
end
```

Program 5.1: (*Continued.*) MATLAB Code for Outer loop.

5.4 INNER LOOP (RATE CONTROL)

The inner iteration loop does the actual quantization of the frequency domain data and in addition performs the rate control. The calculation of the codebook for each sub-region and computation of the number of bits needed to encode the values in the sub-regions are performed in this loop. The Huffman code tables assign shorter code words to smaller quantized values. If the total number of bits resulting from Huffman coding exceeds the number of bits available to encode one frame, the global gain is adjusted to result in a larger quantization step size. The overall steps involved in the inner loop can be seen from the block diagram in Figure 5.5 and the skeletal MATLAB code in Program 5.2.

5.4.1 NON-UNIFORM QUANTIZATION

Layer III uses a non-uniform mid-tread quantizer. Due to the required symmetry, a uniform quantizer with an even number of levels cannot have a reconstruction level at zero. This type of quantizer is referred to as mid-rise quantizer. On the other hand, a mid-tread quantizer that has an odd number of levels will have a reconstruction level at zero. The quantizer raises its input to the 3/4 power before applying the quantizer. This is inverted in the decoder, where the quantized values are re-linearized by raising them to the 4/3 power. This step ensures that the bigger values are quantized with less accuracy than small values, thereby increasing the signal-to-noise ratio at the low level input. The quantization of the vector of spectral values is performed according to the expression

$$ix(i) = nint\left(\left(\frac{|xr(i)|}{\sqrt[4]{2}^{quantizer StepSize}} \right)^{0.75} - 0.0946 \right), \tag{5.5}$$

where xr indicates the frequency lines output from the MDCT module, $ix(i)$ is the quantized value of the input $xr(i)$, i is the index ranging from 0 to 575.

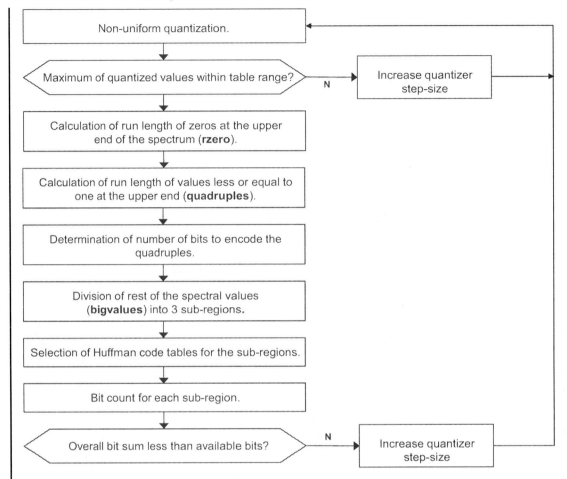

Figure 5.5: Implementation of the Inner Loop (Rate Control).

5.4.2   HUFFMAN CODING

The entropy coding of the quantized frequency lines is performed using Huffman coding. Huffman coding is an entropy encoding algorithm used for lossless data compression. Huffman coding uses a variable-length code table for encoding a source symbol where the code table is derived based on the estimated probability of occurrence for each possible value of the source symbol. In this algorithm, there are 32 Huffman code tables for coding the pairs of quantized values. The major differences between these tables are the maximum value that can be encoded and the signal statistics for which they are optimized. Huffman coding yields a variable length code, i.e., the length of code is varied based on the data statistics. There exists a limit on the maximum quantized value (of the frequency

```
% P 5.2 - Inner Loop

while bits > max_bits

    % dummy flag to simulate an exit controlled "do{}while" loop
    max_l3_enc = 9000;

    % Check if maximum of all quantized values is within the table range
    while max_l3_enc > (8191 + 14)
        cod_info.quantizerStepSize = cod_info.quantizerStepSize + 1.0;
        l3_enc = quantize(xrs, cod_info);
        max_l3_enc = max(l3_enc);
    end

    % Calculate run length of zeros,count1,big_values
    cod_info = calc_runlen(l3_enc, cod_info);

    % Count number of bits to code count1
    [bits cod_info] = count1_bitcount(l3_enc, cod_info);

    % SUBDIVIDE bigvalues
    cod_info = subdivide(cod_info);

    % Codebook Selection for subregion
    cod_info = bigv_tab_select(l3_enc, cod_info);

    % Count number of bits to code subregions
    bits = bits + bigv_bitcount(l3_enc, cod_info );

end
```

Program 5.2: MATLAB Code for Inner loop.

lines) allowed. This forces a constraint on the table size, if a table-lookup is used to requantize the quantized values. Hence, before any processing is carried out, the quantizer step size is increased only until the maximum of the quantized values is within the range of the largest Huffman code table.

The MP3 algorithm delimits the ordered frequency lines into three distinct regions defined by the variables: *rzero*, *count*1 and *bigvalues*. In general, the ordering is by increasing frequency except for the short block mode. In the short block mode, there are three sets of window values in a subband and hence the ordering is done by frequency, then by window and then by scalefactor. The ordering is helpful because large values tend to be at the lower frequencies while long runs of zeros or very small values occur at high frequencies. Dividing the frequency lines into three different regions enables the encoder to encode each region with a different set of Huffman tables specifically tuned for the statistics of that region.

The run length region, $rzero$, identifies and counts the pairs of spectral coefficients in the upper end of the spectrum that are quantized to zero. This region need not be encoded as its size can be easily deduced from the size of the other two regions. The run length of quadruples consists of spectral coefficients equal to -1, 0 or 1 is counted as the region $count1$. Two Huffman code tables are used to encode this region and they code four values at a time. The third region that covers all remaining coefficient values is called the $bigvalues$. The 30 Huffman tables for this region encode the coefficient values in pairs. Figure 5.6 (a) illustrates the unquantized MDCT for a granule of the audio data. Noted that the psychoacoustics module employs a short block for analysis of this granule and the coefficients are reordered for entropy coding. The rate control loop iteratively changes the quantizers until the target rate (128 kbps in this example) is achieved while maintaining the noise floor below the masking threshold. The resulting coefficients are shown in Figure 5.6 (b). It can be observed that some of the low-energy coefficients present at high frequencies are discarded in this process.

There are two Huffman codebooks with the corresponding code length tables to encode the $count1$ region, where one Huffman word is used to encode one of the $count1$ quadruples. The number of bits needed to encode this region is given by

$$bitsum\_count1 = \min(sum_0, sum_1),$$
where
$$sum_0 = \sum_{k=1}^{count1} ht_0\left(ix(4k) + 2ix(4k+1) + 4ix(4k+2) + 8ix(4k+3)\right), \text{ and}$$
$$sum_1 = \sum_{k=1}^{count1} ht_1\left(ix(4k) + 2ix(4k+1) + 4ix(4k+2) + 8ix(4k+3)\right). \tag{5.6}$$

In (5.6) ht_0 and ht_1 refer to the two Huffman code tables that are used to encode the $count1$ region and ix is the set of quantized samples that are encoded. We need to make sure that both the tables include the number of bits needed to encode the sign bits. The table that is selected to encode the $count1$ region is transmitted by the parameter $count1\_select$, which is 0 for ht_0 and 1 for ht_1, respectively.

The pairs of quantized values that are not included in the $rzero$ and $count1$ regions are characterized as the $bigvalues$. The routine $SUBDIVIDE$ further splits the scalefactor bands corresponding to the $bigvalues$ into three regions. The number of scalefactor bands in the first and second regions is contained in $region0\_count$ and $region1\_count$, respectively. The number of bands in the third region can be easily calculated from the $bigvalues$. When a large number of symbols are to be encoded, the construction of an optimal Huffman code table becomes very difficult. Hence, an $ESCAPE$ value is used before coding the frequency lines to improve the coding efficiency.

The tables contain codes for values up to 15 and for values $>=16$, there are two tables provided, in which the largest value 15 is an ESCAPE character. In this case, the value 15 is encoded in an

Figure 5.6: (a) Unquantized MDCT coefficients for a short block. (b) MDCT coefficients (magnitude) quantized to meet target bit rate 128 kbps.

```
% P 5.3 - Calculate run length regions

rzero = 0;
cod_info.count1 = 0 ;

if cod_info.window_switching_flag & cod_info.block_type == 2
   % short blocks
   cod_info.count1 = 0;
    % big_values = 576/2 = 288
   cod_info.big_values = 288;
else
   for i = 576:-2:2
      if ix(i) == 0 & ix(i-1) == 0
         rzero = rzero + 1;
      else
         break
      end
   end

   % If we get all 576/2 = 288 runlength zeros,set big_values = 0
   if rzero == 288
      i = 0;
   end

   while i > 3
      if all(abs(ix(i:-1:i-3))) <= 1)
         cod_info.count1 = cod_info.count1 + 1;
         i = i - 4;
      else
         break;
      end
   end

   cod_info.big_values = i/2;
end
```

Program 5.3: MATLAB Code for calculating the run length regions.

```matlab
% P 5.4 -  Counting number of bits for count1

sum0 = 0;sum1 = 0;
i = cod_info.big_values*2 + 1;
for k = 1:cod_info.count1
   v = abs( ix(i:i+3) );
   i = i + 4;
   p = v(1) + v(2)*2 + v(3)*4 + v(4)*8 + 1;
   signbits = 0;
   % Sign bits are taken into account
   if v(1) ~= 0
      signbits = signbits + 1;
   end
   if v(2) ~= 0
      signbits = signbits + 1;
   end
   if v(3) ~= 0
      signbits = signbits + 1;
   end
   if v(4) ~= 0
      signbits = signbits + 1;
   end
   sum0 = sum0 + signbits;
   sum1 = sum1 + signbits;
   % ht - Huffman tables: 33, 34 are count1-tables
   sum0 = sum0 + ht{33}.hlen(p);
   sum1 = sum1 + ht{34}.hlen(p);
end
if sum0 < sum1
   bitsum_count1 = sum0;
   cod_info.count1table_select = 0;
else
   bitsum_count1 = sum1;
   cod_info.count1table_select = 1;
end
```

Program 5.4: MATLAB Code for counting number of bits for region *count1*.

additional word using a linear PCM code, which has a word length indicated by *linbits*. Figure 5.7 illustrates the main data organization and the Huffman encoding scheme. Thus, by partitioning the MDCT coefficients into regions and sub-regions, error propagation can be well controlled. Within the bitstream, the Huffman codes for the different values are ordered from low to high frequency. Figure 5.8 illustrates the bit usage for encoding different sub-regions in the inner loop. As it can be seen, the inner loop varies the quantization step and continues until the total bit usage is within the bit budget.

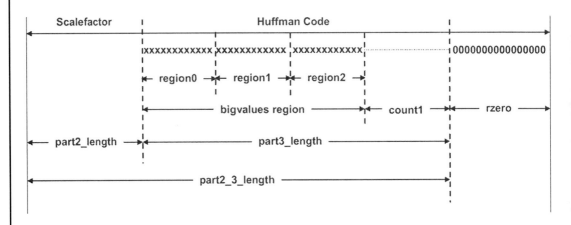

Figure 5.7: Illustration of main data organization and encoding scheme.

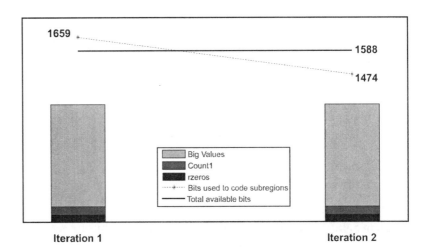

Figure 5.8: Illustration of bit usage in the inner loop.

To summarize, the *global_gain* and the scalefactors are determined by the inner and outer iteration loops. The outer loop shapes the noise spectrum by adjusting the scale factors, while the inner loop determines the *global_gain* that prevents the number of bits to encode the granule exceed *max_bits*.

Figure 5.9 illustrates an example case of the relationship between the number of bits required to encode a granule and the *global_gain*. During initialization, the maximum allowed distortion for

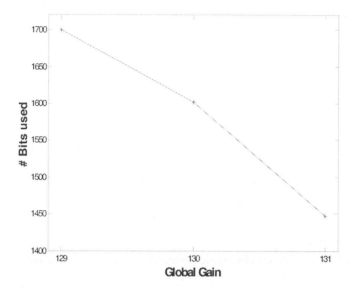

Figure 5.9: Illustration of relationship between *global_gain* and the number of bits required to encode a granule.

each scalefactor band, $xmin$, is determined using the SMR obtained from the psychoacoustic module. During the iteration loop, the scalefactors are increased in small amounts until the quantization noise is below $xmin$ or the scalefactors cannot be modified anymore. Figures 5.10 (a), (b) show the ratio of quantization noise over the allowed distortion at the beginning and end of the outer loop. The number inside the bars indicate the scalefactor values.

5.5   BITSTREAM FORMATTING

The design of the Layer III bitstream fits the encoder's time-varying demand on the coding bits. The encoded data representing the samples do not necessarily fit into a fixed length frame in the encoded bitstream. Instead, a bit reservoir is used with which the encoder can donate bits. Bits are donated when fewer than the average number of bits is required to encode a frame. Similarly, the encoder can borrow bits when needed. Figure 5.12 shows the arrangement of various bit fields in the Layer III bitstream. The bitstream format, which will be again discussed in detail in the decoder section, is described below:

Header: The first 32 bits constitute the header that contains the synchronization and state information. The header information is common to all layers. The layer of the MPEG-1

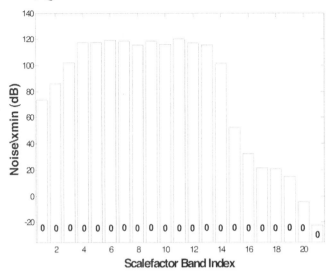

Figure 5.10: (a) Ratio of quantization noise over *xmin* at the start of the outer loop.

encoding algorithm used, bitrate, sampling frequency, mode, copyright, type of de-emphasis used are some of the information it specifies.

CRC: This is a 16 bit parity-check word that is used for optional error protection.

Side Information: Information in the bitstream used for controlling the decoder. Single channel audio frames contain 17 bytes (136 bits) of side information while dual channel audio frames contain 32 bytes (256 bits) of side information.

Main Data: This contains the Huffman encoded information of the audio samples. The *main_data_begin* pointer is used to determine the location of the first bit of the main data in a frame. It also contains the scale factor selection information and a variable, *part2_3_length*, specifying the number of main data bits used. In addition, it contains the information on the block type used in the frame and the Huffman table selection.

Ancillary Data: This is user defined information and need not be necessarily related to the audio stream itself. The number of ancillary bits available can be evaluated from the difference between the available number of bits and the number of bits actually used for the header, side information, error check and main audio data.

5.5.1   BIT RESERVOIR

The effect of pre-echo distortion was discussed in Chapter 3. Consider the case when a period of silence is followed by the sound of a percussive instrument. Such a transient sound requires an increase

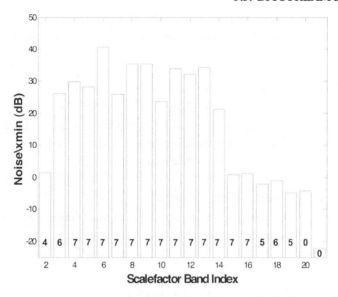

Figure 5.11: (b) Ratio of quantization noise over *xmin* at the end of the outer loop.

HEADER (32)	CRC (0,16)	SIDE INFORMATION (136,256)	MAIN DATA	ANCILLARY BITS

Figure 5.12: Frame Format for Layer III bitstream.

in the number of bits and can cause large quantization errors. These pre-echoes become distinctly audible at low bit rates. The effect of pre-echoes can be mitigated by temporal masking, provided if the transform block size is sufficiently small. Several methodologies have been proposed to mitigate the effect of pre-echoes [112, 113, 114, 115] and using a bit reservoir is one such technique [27, 102].

Although most algorithms are fixed rate, the instantaneous bit rates required to satisfy the masking thresholds in each frame is in general time varying. Bit reservoir is a short-term buffer technique that is used to enhance the coding efficiency of the Huffman coder. The idea is to store surplus bits during periods of low demand and then allocate bits from the reservoir suitably during periods of high demand. This results in a time-varying instantaneous bit rate but a fixed average bit rate. The bit reservoir can provide additional bits which may be used for coding the granule. The number of bits provided is determined within the iteration loops. The main data contains the encoded scale factor and Huffman encode frequency lines. The length of the main data depends on the bitrate. The length of the scalefactor part depends on whether the scalefactors are reused between granules and also on the window length (short or long). The bit reservoir allows unused main data bits stored in one frame to be used by up to two consecutive frames. Hence, the main data are not located necessarily located adjacent to the side information in each frame as shown in Figure 5.13.

In the example illustrated in Figure 5.13, the main data in frame 1 uses bits from frame 0 and frame 1. Frame 2 also uses bits from frame 1 and hence the bits available for frame 2 are totally saved. The next frame, frame 3 requires a large number of bits and hence uses bits from frames 1, 2, and 3. Finally, the frame 4 uses the bits only from frame 4 and is hence self sufficient. Hence, it is observed that, when such a buffering technique is applied, the main data of a particular frame need not be necessarily located adjacent to its side info.

Estimation of Average Number of Bits (*mean_bits*)

The average number of bits per granule is calculated from the frame size. For example, consider the bitrate of 64 kbits/s at sampling rate 48 kHz.

Number of granules = 2.

Bits per frame $= 64,000 \times \frac{1,152}{48,000} = 1,536$ bits.

The header is 4 bytes long and contains information about the layer, bitrate, sampling frequency and stereo mode. The side information takes 17 bytes (136 bits) in single channel mode and contains the necessary information to decode the main data such as Huffman table selection, scalefactors, requantization parameters and window selection.

Side info length + Header= $136 + 32 = 168$ bits.

$\therefore$ Average number of bits $= \dfrac{(\text{Bits per frame} - \text{Side info length})}{\text{Number of granules}} = 684$ bits.

Bit Reservoir Functions

Bits are saved to the reservoir when fewer than the estimated average number of bits is used to encode the granule. If bits are saved for a frame, the size of the reservoir is increased accordingly. The number of bits available for the main data is calculated from the actual estimated threshold (perceptual entropy calculated in the psychoacoustics module), average number of bits and the actual content of the bit reservoir. Initially the maximum size of the reservoir is updated. If the number of bytes available to the inner iteration loop is not used for Huffman encoding, the number is added to the bit reservoir. If the bit reservoir is greater than zero, all bytes exceeding 8 times the maximum allowed content of the bit reservoir are made available for the main data. Program 5.4 illustrates the determination of maximum size of the reservoir.

The maximum bit allowance for each granule is based on the reservoir size at the beginning of that granule and perceptual entropy. First, the number of bits in addition to the average number of bits as demanded by the value of the perceptual entropy of the granule is determined (*more_bits* $= 3.1 PE -$ Average number of bits). If *more_bits* is greater than 100, then

Figure 5.13: Illustration of main data buffer handling.

```matlab
% P 5.5 - Bit Reservoir function

function [] = ResvFrameBegin(fr_ps, mean_bits, bitsPerFrame)
global ResvSize ResvMax;
global l3_side;

if fr_ps.header.version == 1
    mode_gr = 2;
    resvLimit = 4088; % main_data_begin has 9 bits in MPEG 1
else
    mode_gr = 1;
    resvLimit = 2040; % main_data_begin has 8 bits in MPEG 2
end;

% main_data_begin was set by the formatter to the expected value fc
%the next call -- this should agree with our reservoir size
expectedResvSize = l3_side.main_data_begin * 8;
fullFrameBits = mean_bits*mode_gr;

% Determine maximum size of reservoir: ResvMax + frameLength <= 768
if bitsPerFrame > 7680
    ResvMax = 0;
else
    ResvMax = 7680 - bitsPerFrame;
end

% Limit max size to resvLimit bits because main_data_begin cannot
% indicate a larger value
if ResvMax > resvLimit
    ResvMax = resvLimit;
end
```

Program 5.4: MATLAB Code to update maximum size of the reservoir.

max (*more_bits*/8, 6 * *Reservoir_Size*) bytes are taken from the bit reservoir and made available for the main data, in addition to the average number of bits. Program 5.5 demonstrates this computation.

After the loop computations are complete, the number of bytes not used for the main data are added to the bit reservoir and hence the reservoir size is adjusted to reflect the granule's usage. Figure 5.14 illustrates the bit availability for coding each granule of the data frames. As described earlier, the total bit availability depends on the bit reservoir size at each stage.

```
% P 5.6 - Bit allocation for each granule

function [max_bits] = ResvMaxBits(fr_ps, pe, mean_bits)
global l3_side;
global ResvSize ResvMax;

mean_bits = mean_bits/fr_ps.stereo;
max_bits = fix(mean_bits);
if max_bits > 4095
   max_bits = 4095;
end
if ResvMax == 0
   return;
end

% Compute more_bits
more_bits = fix(pe * 3.1 - mean_bits);
add_bits = 0;

if more_bits > 100
   % check if frac is integer
   frac = fix((ResvSize*6)/10);

   if frac < more_bits
      add_bits = frac;
   else
      add_bits = more_bits;
   end
end

over_bits = fix(ResvSize - ((ResvMax*8)/10) - add_bits);

if over_bits > 0
   add_bits = add_bits + over_bits;
end

max_bits = max_bits + add_bits;

if max_bits > 4095
   max_bits = 4095;
end
```

Program 5.5: MATLAB Code to calculate bit allocation for each granule.

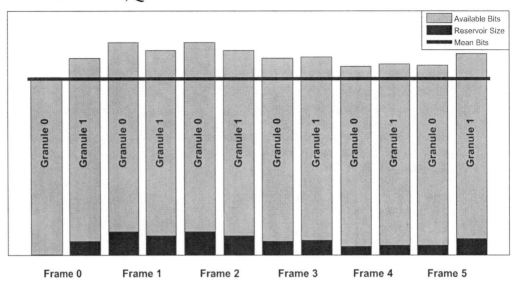

Figure 5.14: Illustration of total available bits to encode data frames.

5.6   SUMMARY

This chapter presented a detailed overview of the bit allocation strategies used in the MP3 algorithm and provides details on the bitstream formatting performed at the encoder. The use of short blocks in the MDCT module enables temporal pre-masking of pre-echoes during transients; longer blocks during steady-state periods improve coding gain, while also reducing side information and hence the overall bit rate. Bit allocation and quantization of the spectral lines are realized in a nested loop procedure that uses both lossy non-uniform quantization and lossless Huffman coding. The inner loop adjusts the non-uniform quantizer step sizes for each block until the number of bits required to encode the transform components falls within the bit budget. The outer loop evaluates the quality of the coded signal (analysis-by-synthesis) in terms of quantization noise relative to the JND thresholds. The use of a bit reservoir enables this perceptual coding algorithm to achieve a time-varying instantaneous bit rate but a fixed average bit rate. The reader is directed to [27, 89, 102, 103] for further details on bit allocation strategies and the bit reservoir usage.

CHAPTER 6

Decoder

The MP3 decoder operates on the encoded (received) bitstream to reconstruct the PCM audio data. The basic block diagram of the decoder is illustrated in Figure 6.1. This design shows the decoding of the single channel case and can be easily scaled for the stereo decoder. The contents of the Layer III Bitstream are organized into frames and each frame contains the necessary information to reconstruct the original PCM audio samples. A frame as explained in Section 5.5 consists of 5 parts: the header, CRC, side information, main data and ancillary data. In the following sections we will describe in detail the different steps involved in the decoding process.

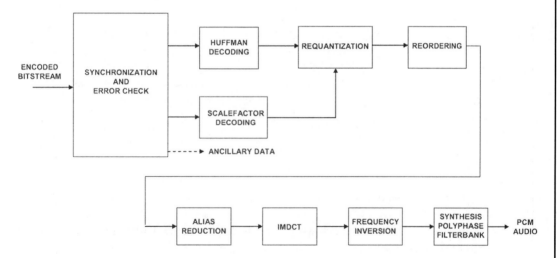

Figure 6.1: Block diagram of the MP3 decoder.

6.1 SYNCHRONIZATION AND ERROR CHECKING

This is the first unit of the decoder that receives the encoded bitstream, identifies and extracts the contents of the bitstream and transmits the information to the other blocks of the decoder. In addition to describing the operations performed in this module, a detailed analysis of the bitstream format is also presented in this section.

The illustration of the bitstream format of a Layer III frame can be found in Figure 5.5. The header part of the frame contains a 12-bit synchronization word and the system information.

Each frame starts with this 12-bit synchronization word and the decoder detects the beginning of a new frame using this information. The remaining part of the header specifies the layer used in the frame, the bitrate used for transmission, the sampling frequency, whether the coded audio signal is a single channel or dual channel and some additional information related to the system. We cannot completely avoid spurious synchronization words from appearing in other parts of the frame. Therefore, in practice, to obtain a stable synchronization, all the bits in the header that are already known in advance by the decoder should be used as the synchronization word.

The MP3 encoder provides an optional error detection feature for each frame using a 16-bit CRC check word. The CRC word is placed in the bit positions 16 to 31 of the header and side information (see Figure 6.2). The encoder ensures that only the most sensitive information in each

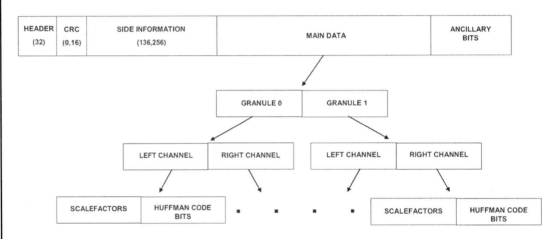

Figure 6.2: Organization of scalefactors and Huffman coded data.

frame is included in the CRC check word. This is due to that fact that any error in these values can corrupt the entire frame whereas errors in the main data will corrupt only a part of the frame. The Hamming distance of the CRC check work is $d = 4$, which detects up to 3 single bit errors or an error burst of up to 16 bits. If the *protection bit* in the header is equal to 0, it indicates that a CRC check word has been inserted in the bitstream by the encoder just after the header. The error detection method used has a generator polynomial of the form

$$G(x) = x^{16} + x^{15} + x^2 + 1 .$$
(6.1)

The CRC check diagram is shown in Figure 6.3. The shift register has the initial state '1111 1111 1111 1111' and the data bits to be included to the CRC check are fed as inputs to the circuit. For every bit of the data, the shift register is shifted by one bit. After the shift operations are complete, the output bits $b_{15}...b_0$ constitute a word to be compared to the CRC check word in the bitstream. A transmission error in the protected field is detected if the words are not identical. If the frame is corrupted, the common practice is to mute the actual frame or repeat the previous frame if it was free of errors.

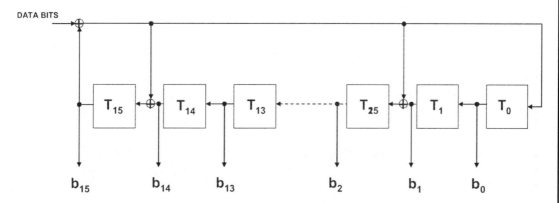

Figure 6.3: CRC check diagram.

The Synchronization and Error Checking module receives the incoming bitstream and identifies the location of each frame. If location of a frame is known, it is possible for the succeeding blocks in the decoder to extract all information contained in the frame. The decoder begins by searching for the 12-bit synchronization word in the bitstream. The validity of the word is tested by reading the header information and performing CRC check on the header and side information, if available. The synchronization word can be discarded if the CRC fails and search for a new synchronization word begins.

The MATLAB code section in Program 6.1 lists the steps involved in seeking the synchronization word in the bitstream. The code section in Program 6.2 shows the different parameters extracted from the header information in the bitstream.

6.2   DECODING SIDE INFORMATION

The side information section of the bitstream contains the necessary information to decode the main data. In particular, it contains the information pertaining to the Huffman tables to be used during the Huffman decoding process and the information for reconstruction of the scalefactors. The side information also contains the pointer to the beginning of main data, i.e., the location where the main data actually begins. For a single channel, the side information is 136 bits, while 256 bits are used for a dual channel (stereo).

6.2.1   EXTRACTING PARAMETERS FOR HUFFMAN DECODING

Though not shown explicitly in Figure 6.1, prior to performing Huffman decoding, the decoder needs to extract the necessary parameters from the side information. Therefore, the first step is to

```
% P 6.1 - Seek the synchronization word and place the bitstream poin

function [bs, retval] = seek_sync(bs, sync, N)

global ALIGNING
maxi = round(2^N - 1);
aligning = rem(bs.totbit, ALIGNING);

if (aligning)
    [bs val] = getbits(bs, (ALIGNING-aligning));
end

[bs val] = getbits(bs, N);

while (bitand(val, maxi) ~= sync) & ~(bs.eobs)
    val = bitshift(val, ALIGNING);
    [bs v] = getbits(bs, ALIGNING);
    val = bitor(val, v);
end
if bs.eobs
    retval = 0;
else
    retval = 1;
end
```

Program 6.1: MATLAB Code to seek synchronization word.

identify where to find the Huffman code bits in the bitstream and also determine which Huffman tables need to be used. The decoder has to also find whether ESCAPE values are present in the Huffman code bits (refer to Section 5.4.2 for details). The other important task here is to ensure that irrespective of the number of frequency lines represented by the Huffman code bits, 576 frequency lines are generated when the decoding actually occurs. If this requirement is not satisfied, the frame is filled by zero padding.

6.2.2   EXTRACTING PARAMETERS FOR SCALEFACTOR DECODING

The main data section of the bitstream contains the encoded scalefactor values and the Huffman coded data. The beginning of the main data is determined by a pointer placed in the side information bits. The length of the pointer is 9 bits and the bit reservoir cannot exceed the value $8\left(2^9 - 1\right) = 4088$ bits. The variable *part2_length* contains the number of bits in the main data that are used for the scalefactors and the variable *part2_3_length* contains the total number of bits used by the scalefactors and the Huffman coded data. Hence, these values are used to determine the location of the scalefactors, main data and the ancillary data, if available. As seen in the encoder sections, the scale factor selection information needs to be considered during scalefactor decoding. For the bands

```
% P 6.2 - Decode the header information from the bitstream

function [bs, fr_ps] = decode_info(bs, fr_ps)

[bs fr_ps.header.version] = get1bit(bs);

[bs val] = getbits(bs,2);
fr_ps.header.lay = 4-val;

[bs val] = get1bit(bs);
fr_ps.header.error_protection = ~val; % error protect. TRUE/FALSE

[bs val] = getbits(bs,4);
fr_ps.header.bitrate_index = val;

[bs val] = getbits(bs,2);
fr_ps.header.sampling_frequency = val;

[bs val] = get1bit(bs);
fr_ps.header.padding = val;

[bs val] = get1bit(bs);
fr_ps.header.extension = val;

[bs val] = getbits(bs,2);
fr_ps.header.mode = val;
[bs val] = getbits(bs,2);
fr_ps.header.mode_ext = val;

[bs val] = get1bit(bs);
fr_ps.header.copyright = val;

[bs val] = get1bit(bs);
fr_ps.header.original = val;

[bs val] = getbits(bs,2);
fr_ps.header.emphasis = val;
```

Program 6.2: MATLAB Code to decode header information.

in which *scfsi* is set to '1', the scalefactors in the first granule are used for the second granule also. If it is set to '0', different scalefactors are to be used. The other important parameters that need to be known are the length of the scalefactors for the different bands (*slen1* and *slen2*). This can be determined from the variable *scalefac_compress* extracted from the side information bit sequence. Program 6.3 illustrates the extraction of some of the parameters from the side information bit sequence that will be used for scalefactor and Huffman decoding.

```
% P 6.3 - Extracting parameters from Side Information.

% These will be used for scalefactor and Huffman Decoding
[bs si.main_data_begin] = getbits(bs, 8);

if (stereo == 1)
    [bs si.private_bits] = getbits(bs,1);
else
    [bs si.private_bits] = getbits(bs,2);
end

for gr = 1:1
    for ch = 1:stereo
        [bs si.ch(ch).gr(gr).part2_3_length] = getbits(bs, 12);
        [bs si.ch(ch).gr(gr).big_values] = getbits(bs, 9);
        [bs si.ch(ch).gr(gr).global_gain] = getbits(bs, 8);
        [bs si.ch(ch).gr(gr).scalefac_compress] = getbits(bs, 9);
        [bs si.ch(ch).gr(gr).window_switching_flag] = get1bit(bs);

        if (si.ch(ch).gr(gr).window_switching_flag)
            [bs si.ch(ch).gr(gr).block_type] = getbits(bs, 2);
            [bs si.ch(ch).gr(gr).mixed_block_flag] = get1bit(bs);

            [bs si.ch(ch).gr(gr).table_select(1)] = getbits(bs, 5)
            [bs si.ch(ch).gr(gr).table_select(2)] = getbits(bs, 5)

            [bs si.ch(ch).gr(gr).subblock_gain(1)] = getbits(bs, 3
            [bs si.ch(ch).gr(gr).subblock_gain(2)] = getbits(bs, 3
            [bs si.ch(ch).gr(gr).subblock_gain(3)] = getbits(bs, 3
```

Program 6.3: MATLAB Code to extract some of the parameters from side information.

6.3   SCALEFACTOR DECODING

The purpose of the scalefactor decoding block in Figure 6.1 is to decode the scalefactors, which form the first part of the main data. The parameters extracted from the side information are input to this block along with the encoded scalefactors. The decoded scalefactors are returned by this module, which will in turn be used during the requantization process. The organization of scalefactors within a frame of data is shown in Figure 6.2. As seen in the figure, each frame of data is split into two granules and for each granule, the scalefactors and the Huffman coded data are presented for the two channels separately.

As described in Section 5.2, the scalefactors are decoded according to the *slen1* and *slen2* which themselves ate determined from the values of *scalefac_compress*. The decoded values can be used as entries into a table or used to calculate the factors for each scalefactor band directly. When decoding the second granule, the *scfsi* has to be considered. As described in the previous section, the side information contains the information to decode the scalefactors. Each of the scalefactors transmitted, applies for one scalefactor band. The number of scalefactor bands and also the number of scalefactors transmitted depends on the type of the window used in the MDCT module of the encoder. A scalefactor band in Layer III indicates a set of frequency lines which are scaled by the same scalefactor. In general, there are 21 scalefactor bands at each sampling frequency in a granule for the case of long windows (types 0,1 or 3) and 12 bands in the case of short windows (type 2). Hence, there can be a maximum of 36 scalefactors for a channel within a granule and this situation arises when three short windows are used prior to the MDCT module. The total number of scalefactors for a channel must be known before the decoding process.

The MATLAB code sections Program 6.4 (a) and 6.4 (b) describe the steps to decode the scalefactors for the cases when short and long windows are used in the granule during encoding, respectively. In Layer III, the variable *scfsi_band* is used to apply the scalefactor selection informa-

```
% P 6.4(a) - Obtain scalefactors for the case of Short Windows (type 2)
for i = 1:2
    for sfb = sfbtable.s(i)+1:sfbtable.s(i+1)+1
        for window = 1:3
            scalefac(ch).s(window, sfb) = hgetbits(slen(i,
                              gr_info.scalefac_compress+1));
        end
    end
end
sfb=13;
window = 1:3;
scalefac(ch).s(window, sfb) = 0;
```

Program 6.4: (a): MATLAB Code to get the scalefactors (Case for short windows).

tion, $scfsi$, to groups of scalefactor bands instead of a single scalefactor band. The application of scalefactors to the granules is controlled by the $scfsi$. For long windows with a total of 21 scalefactor bands, the variable *scfsi_band*, allows 4 groups of scalefactor bands, as can be seen in Program 6.4 (b). If the block type is switched to a short window for one of the granules, separate scalefactors are transmitted for each granule in the frame.

```
% P 6.4(b) - Obtain scalefactors for the case of Long Windows (types
0,1,or 3)
for i = 1:4
    if (si.ch(ch).scfsi(i) == 0) | (gr == 0+1)
        for sfb = sfbtable.l(i)+1:sfbtable.l(i+1)
            if i < 3
                scalefac(ch).l(sfb) = hgetbits(slen(1,
                                        gr_info.scalefac_compress+1));
            else
                scalefac(ch).l(sfb) = hgetbits(slen(2,
                                        gr_info.scalefac_compress+1));
            end
        end
    end
end
scalefac(ch).l(23) = 0;
```

Program 6.4: (b): MATLAB Code to obtain the scalefactors (Case for long windows).

6.4   HUFFMAN DECODING

The purpose of this block is to decode the Huffman code bits from the main data. Individual code words in the incoming Huffman code are not separated. Hence, a single code word in the middle of the code bits cannot be identified without actually decoding from the start of the code word. As a result, an error occurring somewhere in the Huffman code bits will make it very difficult to decode the remaining bits. All the necessary information bits to decode the Huffman coded bits are obtained from the side information as explained earlier. The *bigvalues* are decoded first using the tables indicated by *table_select*. The frequency lines in the regions *region0*, *region1* and *region2* are decoded in pairs until the number of pairs reaches the value specified by *bigvalues*. The value *count1* is the number of quadruples of decoded values and can be determined from *count1table_select*. The remaining Huffman code bits are then decoded using the table specified by *count1table_select*. The decoding is performed until all bits have been decoded or the quantized values for 576 frequency lines have been decoded. If there are more coded bits used than necessary to decode 576 lines, they are discarded.

As described in Section 5.4.2, ESCAPE values are introduced during Huffman coding at the encoder. When quantized frequency lines exceed the value 15, only the value 15 is encoded. The remaining information is represented in the Huffman code bits as an ESCAPE value. Hence, the Huffman decoder must detect the presence of ESCAPE values and sign bits too, in order to reconstruct the quantized frequency lines. Program 6.5 shows the MATLAB code section illustrates the overall Huffman decoding process.

```
% P 6.5 - Huffman Decoding

%Find region boundary for short block case

if si.ch(ch).gr(gr).window_switching_flag &
                        si.ch(ch).gr(gr).block_type == 2
    % Region2
    region1Start = 36;
    region2Start = 576;   % No Region2 for short block case
else
% Find region boundary for long block case
    region1Start = sfBandIndex(sfreq).l(si.ch(ch).gr(gr).region0_count
                            +1+1);
    region2Start = sfBandIndex(sfreq).l(si.ch(ch).gr(gr).region0_count +
                            si.ch(ch).gr(gr).region1_count +2+1);
end

grBits     = part2_start + si.ch(ch).gr(gr).part2_3_length;
currentBit = totbit;

% Read big_values
for i = 0:2:si.ch(ch).gr(gr).big_values*2-1
    if   i < region1Start
       h = ht(si.ch(ch).gr(gr).table_select(1)+1);
    elseif i < region2Start
       h = ht(si.ch(ch).gr(gr).table_select(2)+1);
    else
       h = ht(si.ch(ch).gr(gr).table_select(3)+1);
    end

    [error x y v w] = huffman_decoder(h);
    is(floor(i/SSLIMIT)+1, rem(i, SSLIMIT)+1) = x;
    is(floor((i+1)/SSLIMIT)+1, rem((i+1), SSLIMIT) +1) = y;
end
grBits     = part2_start + si.ch(ch).gr(gr).part2_3_length;
currentBit = totbit;
```

Program 6.5: MATLAB Code to perform Huffman decoding. (*Continues.*)

```
% Read count1 area
h = ht(si.ch(ch).gr(gr).count1table_select+32+1);

i = si.ch(ch).gr(gr).big_values*2;
while (totbit < part2_start + si.ch(ch).gr(gr).part2_3_length ) & i <
                                                        SSLIMIT*SBLIM
    [error x y v w] = huffman_decoder(h);
    is(floor(i/SSLIMIT)+1, rem(i, SSLIMIT)+1) = v;
    is(floor((i+1)/SSLIMIT)+1, rem((i+1), SSLIMIT)+1) = w;
    is(floor((i+2)/SSLIMIT)+1, rem((i+2), SSLIMIT)+1) = x;
    is(floor((i+3)/SSLIMIT)+1, rem((i+3), SSLIMIT)+1) = y;
    i = i + 4;
end

grBits     = part2_start + si.ch(ch).gr(gr).part2_3_length;
currentBit = totbit;

if totbit > part2_start + si.ch(ch).gr(gr).part2_3_length
    i = i- 4;
    rewindNbits(totbit - part2_start - si.ch(ch).gr(gr).part2_3_length
end

% Dismiss stuffing Bits
grBits     = part2_start + si.ch(ch).gr(gr).part2_3_length;
currentBit = totbit;

if currentBit < grBits
    hgetbits(grBits - currentBit);
end
```

Program 6.5: (*Continued.*) MATLAB Code to perform Huffman decoding.

6.5   REQUANTIZATION

The primary purpose of the requantization is to generate a perceptually identical copy of the frequency lines as generated by the MDCT block in the encoder. This is done through a descaling operation which is based on the scaled quantized frequency lines obtained from the Huffman decoder module and the scalefactors extracted from the scalefactor decoder. The non-uniform quantizer at the encoder uses a power law and hence the frequency line, is, from the Huffman decoder are raised to the power 4/3. This is the inverse power of that used in the encoder. This is either done using a table lookup or by explicitly calculating it. The calculation of the frequency lines belonging to one channel within a granule for the cases of long and short windows are shown in (6.2) and (6.3). Given the Huffman decoded values is_i, at buffer index i, the input to the synthesis filter bank, for the case of long windows is given by

$$xr_i = \frac{sign(is_i)\,|is_i|^{\frac{4}{3}}\,2^{\frac{1}{4}(global\_gain[gr]-210)}}{2^{(scalefac\_multiplier(scalefac\_l[sfb][ch][gr]+preflag[gr].pretab[sfb]))}} \,. \tag{6.2}$$

Similarly, the frequency channels within a granule for the case of short windows can be computed as

$$xr_i = \frac{sign(is_i)\,|is_i|^{\frac{4}{3}}\,2^{\frac{1}{4}(global\_gain[gr]-210-8.subblock\_gain[window][gr])}}{2^{(scalefac\_multiplier.scalefac\_s[gr][ch][sfb][window])}} \,. \tag{6.3}$$

It can be observed from Equations (6.2) and (6.3) that the parameters *global_gain* and *sub-block_gain* (in the case of short windows) affect all the values within a time window. Note that the scalefactors and *preflag* adjust the gain within each scalefactor band. The *global_gain* defines the quantization step size used for one channel within a granule. The constant '210' used in these two expressions is a system constant needed to scale the output appropriately. The scalefactors are logarithmically quantized in the encoder which can be identified using the *scalefac_scale* flag. The value for *scalefac_multiplier* is determined based on the value of this flag. The variables *pretab* and *preflag* are used only in the case of long windows and they were applied in the MDCT module at the encoder. The variable *pretab* specifies a single value per scalefactor band that is used for preemphasis. The parameter *preflag* that is added to the scalefactors is used for additional amplification of the higher frequencies. The scalefactors *scalefac_l* and *scalefac_s* for the cases of long and short windows, respectively, are determined by the scalefactor decoder block. In the case of short windows, a gain factor specified by the parameter *subblock_gain* can be obtained from the side information. Program 6.6 illustrates a part of the MATLAB code section for the requantization in the Layer III decoder.

6.6   REORDERING

After requantization, the frequency lines generated are not always ordered the same way. In the MDCT block at the encoder, if a long window (Figure 4.2) is used prior to transformation, the frequency lines generated would be ordered first by subband and then by frequency. However, using short windows would generate frequency lines first ordered by subband, then by window and at last by frequency. However, to improve the efficiency of the Huffman coding, the frequency lines for the short windows (three overlapped) are reordered first by subband, then by frequency and finally by the window type. The purpose of this reordering step is to detect if short windows have been applied to either of the subbands and reorder the values appropriately. The variables *window_switching_flag* and *block_type* obtained from the side information are used to determine if the reordering step is needed. The sample code section for performing reordering in the case of short blocks is shown in Program 6.7.

```
% P 6.6 - Requantization step

% This does not show the entire code for performing requantization.
illustrates few important steps.

% Compute overall (global) scaling.
xr(sb+1, ss+1) = 2.0^(0.25 * (gr_info.global_gain - 210.0));

%    Do long/short dependent scaling operations.
if (gr_info.window_switching_flag & ...
        (((gr_info.block_type == 2) & (gr_info.mixed_block_flag == 0
        ((gr_info.block_type == 2) & gr_info.mixed_block_flag & (sb
                                                                   2))
    xr(sb+1, ss+1) = xr(sb+1, ss+1) * power(2.0, 0.25*-8.0*
        gr_info.subblock_gain(floor((sb*18+ss-cb_begin)/cb_width)+1

    xr(sb+1, ss+1) = xr(sb+1, ss+1)* power(2.0, 0.25*-2.0*
            (1.0+gr_info.scalefac_scale)*scalefac(ch).s(floor((sb*18+
                                        cb_begin)/cb_width)+1, cb)

else
% LONG block types 0,1,3 & 1st 2 subbands of switched blocks
    xr(sb+1, ss+1) = xr(sb+1, ss+1) * ...
        power(2.0, -0.5*(1.0+gr_info.scalefac_scale)* ...
        ( scalefac(ch).l(cb)+gr_info.preflag*pretab(cb) ));
end

% Scale quantized value
if is(sb+1, ss+1) < 0
    sign = 1;
else
    sign = 0;
end
xr(sb+1, ss+1) = xr(sb+1, ss+1) * ...
    power( double(abs(is(sb+1, ss+1))), double(4.0/3.0) );

if sign
    xr(sb+1, ss+1) = -xr(sb+1, ss+1);
end
```

Program 6.6: MATLAB Code illustrating the steps in requantization.

```
% P 6.7 - Reordering step

% This does not show the entire code for performing reordering. It
illustrates a few important steps, when the window is purely short

sfb_start = 0;
sfb_lines = sfBandIndex(sfreq).s(2);

for sfb = 1:13
    for window = 0:2
        for freq = 1:sfb_lines
            src_line = sfb_start*3 + window*sfb_lines + freq;
            des_line = (sfb_start*3) + window + (freq*3);
            ro(ceil(des_line/SSLIMIT), rem(des_line, SSLIMIT)+1) = ..
                xr(ceil(src_line/SSLIMIT), rem(src_line, SSLIMIT)+1);
        end
    end
    sfb_start = sfBandIndex(sfreq).s(sfb);
    sfb_lines = sfBandIndex(sfreq).s(sfb+1) - sfb_start;
end
```

Program 6.7: MATLAB Code illustrating reordering.

6.7   ALIAS RECONSTRUCTION

In Section 4.2.2, it was described that an alias reduction was applied after performing the MDCT. In order to obtain a correction reconstruction of the PCM audio, the aliasing artifacts must be added to the signal again at the decoder. The alias reconstruction involves eight butterfly calculations for each subband as shown in Figure 6.5. Figure 6.4 illustrates the alias reduction butterfly for the decoder. The coefficients cs and ca can be obtained as described in Equation (4.3). The MATLAB code section illustrating the alias reconstruction process is shown in Program 6.8. It can be observed that the indices of the array **xr** indicate the frequency lines in a granule, arranged in the order of lowest to the highest frequency (zero being the lowest and 575 the highest). Similar to the case of the encoder, alias reduction is not applied for granules that use short blocks.

6.8   THE INVERSE MODIFIED DISCRETE COSINE TRANSFORM

The frequency lines from the alias reconstruction block are processed using the IMDCT block and mapped to the polyphase filter subband samples. The analytical expression of the IMDCT is given

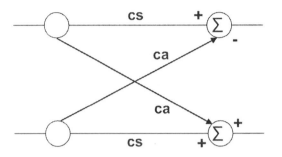

Figure 6.4: Alias reduction butterfly for the decoder.

by

$$x_i = \sum_{k=0}^{\frac{n}{2}-1} X_k \cos\left(\frac{\pi}{2n}(2i + 1 + n/2)(2k + 1)\right), \text{ for } i = 0 \text{ to } n - 1, \tag{6.4}$$

where the frequency lines are denoted by X_k and n is 12 for short blocks and 36 for long blocks. The different types of windows used in the MDCT window switching are shown in Figure 4.2. For all block types other than short blocks, the result x_i is multiplied with the appropriate window. When the block type is *short*, the window is multiplied to each of the three blocks in the subband, and these windowed short blocks are then overlapped and concatenated. The result of these calculations is a vector for each subband. These vectors are then overlapped with half a window and added, resulting in 32 subband vectors, S_i. The first half of the block of 36 values is overlapped with the second half of the previous block. The second half of the current block is stored for use in the next block. The overlap-add operation used in the IMDCT module is illustrated in Figure 6.5. The MATLAB code for the implementation of the IMDCT module is illustrated in Program 6.9.

6.9 POLYPHASE SYNTHESIS FILTERBANK

In order to compensate for frequency inversions of the synthesis polyphase filter bank, every odd time sample of every odd subband is multiplied with -1. To summarize, the frequency lines are preprocessed by the alias reduction method described in Section 6.7 and fed into the IMDCT matrix (each 18 into one transform block). The first half of the output values are added to the stored overlap values from the last block. These values are the new output values and are input values for the polyphase filterbank. The second half of the output values is stored for overlap with the next data granule. For every second subband of the polyphase filterbank, every second input value is multiplied by -1 to correct for the frequency inversion of the polyphase filterbank. The algorithm for computing the polyphase filter bank is illustrated in Program 6.10. Once the samples from each of the 32 subbands have been calculated, they are applied to the synthesis polyphase filter bank.

```
% P 6.8 - Decoder anti-aliasing butterflies

% More specifically, they are the %'aliasing' butterflies, that
recreate the aliasing caused by the analysis filterbank

function [hybridIn] = III_antialias(xr, gr_info)
% Globals for IMDCT
global ca cs;
global SBLIMIT SSLIMIT;

% clear all inputs
hybridIn = xr;
if  gr_info.window_switching_flag & gr_info.block_type == 2 & ...
        ~gr_info.mixed_block_flag
    return;
end
if gr_info.window_switching_flag & gr_info.mixed_block_flag & ...
        gr_info.block_type == 2
    sblim = 1+1;
else
    sblim = SBLIMIT-1;
end
% 31 alias-reduction operations between each pair of sub-bands
% with 8 butterflies between each pair
ss = 0:7;
for sb = 1:sblim
    bu = xr(sb, 18-ss);
    bd = xr(sb+1, ss+1);
    hybridIn(sb, 18-ss) = bu.*cs(ss+1) - bd.*ca(ss+1);
    hybridIn(sb+1, ss+1) = bd.*cs(ss+1) + bu.*ca(ss+1);
end
```

Program 6.8: MATLAB Code illustrating alias reconstruction.

The synthesis polyphase filter bank transforms the 32 subband blocks of 18 samples each in each granule into 18 blocks of 32 PCM samples. In the synthesis operation, the 32 subband values are transformed to the vector $\mathbf{V}$, using a variant of the IMDCT (matrixing). Then, $\mathbf{V}$ is pushed into a FIFO which can store 16 vectors. The vector $\mathbf{U}$ is created from the alternate 32 component blocks in the FIFO and a window function $\mathbf{D}$ is applied to $\mathbf{U}$ to compute $\mathbf{W}$. The reconstructed samples are obtained from the $\mathbf{W}$ vector by decomposing it into 16 blocks each containing 32 samples and summing these blocks. The window function $\mathbf{D}$, is illustrated in Figure 6.6 and the implementation of the synthesis polyphase filter bank is shown in Figure 6.7.

Figure 6.5: Overlap add operation used in the IMDCT module.

Figure 6.6: Window function, D, for the synthesis filter bank.

```
% P 6.9 - IMDCT: Inverse Modified Discrete Cosine Transform

function [out] = imdct(in, blk_type)
global win cos_i;
out  = zeros(1, 36);
tmp = zeros(1, 12);

% type 2: short block
if blk_type == 2
   N = 12; m = 0:N/2-1;
   for i = 1:3
      for p = 0:N-1
         tmp(p+1) = (cos(pi/(2*N)*(2*p+1+N/2)*(2*m+1))*in(i+3*m)) *
                    win(blk_type+1, p+1);
      end
      out(6*i+1:6*i+N) = out(6*i+1:6*i+N) + tmp(1:N);
   end
else
   N = 36; m = 0:N/2-1;
   for p = 0:N-1
      out(p+1) = (cos_i(rem((2*p+1+N/2)*(2*m+1), 4*36)+1)*in(m+1)) *
                 win(blk_type+1, p+1);
   end
end
```

Program 6.9: MATLAB Code illustrating IMDCT.

6.10 SUMMARY

In this chapter, a detailed description of the design of a MPEG-1 Layer III audio decoder was presented. The decoder deciphers the received bitstream, restores the quantized subband values and reconstructs the audio signal from the subband values. The primary advantage of this decoder is the simplicity of its implementation, since it just reconstructs the bitstream and does not consider the psychoacoustics model or the quality of the encoded data. In fact, it is simple enough to allow single-chip, real-time decoder implementations. The encoded bitstream also supports an optional cyclic redundancy check (CRC) error detection code. Though the MPEG-1 Layer III coder is lossy, this algorithm aims at providing a perceptually lossless compression. The reader in need of additional details on the decoder implementation is referred to [116, 117, 118].

```
% P 6.10 - Subband synthesis

function [synth32, clip] = SubBandSynthesis(w, chn)

global SBLIMIT HAN_SIZE y D N
global SCALE
clip = 0;
synth32 = zeros(1, SBLIMIT);
y(chn, 2*HAN_SIZE:-1:65) = y(chn, 2*HAN_SIZE-64:-1:1);

for i = 1:64
   y(chn, i) = N(i, 1:SBLIMIT)*w;
end

i = 0:15;
i = bitshift(i+1, -1, 16)*64;
for j = 1:32
   k = j:32:512;
   l = k + i;
   synth32(j) = sum(D(k).*y(chn, l));
% Casting truncates towards zero for both positive and negative numbe
   if  synth32(j) > 0
      foo = fix(synth32(j)*double(SCALE));
   else
      foo = fix(synth32(j)*double(SCALE));
   end

   if foo >=  fix(SCALE)
      synth32(j) = fix(SCALE-1);
      clip = clip + 1;
   elseif foo <  fix(-SCALE)
      synth32(j) = fix(-SCALE);
      clip = clip + 1;
   else
      synth32(j) = foo;
   end
end
```

Program 6.10: MATLAB Code illustrating polyphase synthesis filterbank.

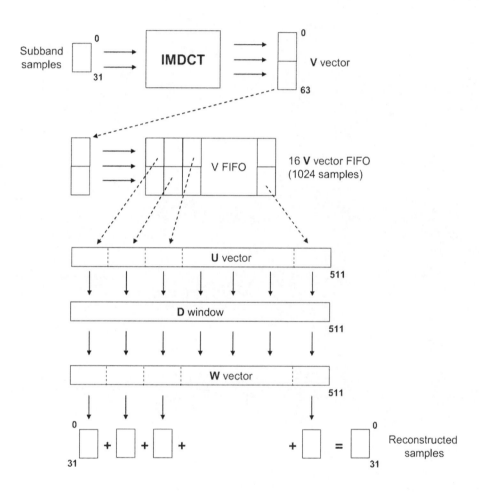

Figure 6.7: Polyphase implementation of the synthesis filter bank [78].

APPENDIX A

Complexity Profile of the MPEG-1 Layer III Algorithm

Analysis of the computational complexity of the MP3 encoder and decoder is essential in understanding the behavior of the algorithm. The complexity profile for any algorithm is highly dependent on the platform used for the implementation (C, MATLAB), operating system and the underlying hardware architecture. The choice of a suitable platform for implementing algorithms is based on different factors such as the speed of execution, availability of advanced libraries, visualization capabilities and flexibility for testing. In this chapter, the complexity analysis of both the C implementation (ISO dist-10) and the MATLAB implementation are presented. MATLAB is a high level double-precision floating-point engine that provides a highly advanced and flexible interface for testing and visualization. On the flip side, execution is slower than the more traditional compiled binaries and libraries.

As illustrated in Figure A.1 the MATLAB implementation of the MPEG-1 algorithm incurs much higher complexity at the encoder in comparison to the decoder. As described earlier, the decoder

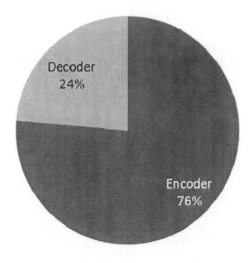

Figure A.1: Complexity Profile of MATLAB implementation of the MPEG-1 Layer III algorithm.

is simple enough to allow single-chip, real-time implementations. The complexity at the encoder can be attributed primarily to the extensive amount of bit-manipulation routines involved.

Figure A.2 illustrates the complexity profiles of the MATLAB and C implementations of the MP3 algorithm. Bit-manipulation operations, nested for-loops and dynamic memory allocation are very expensive in MATLAB. Therefore, the rate-control loop takes up most of the computational horsepower at the encoder. Most of the remaining processing bandwidth is used up in the bitstream formatting. At the decoder, Huffman decoding is costly in terms of bit-manipulation and, as expected, is the most expensive part of the algorithm. In contrast, the C implementation is very efficient in bit-wise processing and hence the complexity of the psychoacoustics model and the subband analysis are comparable to that of the rate control loop. Figure A.3 shows the complexity profiles of the rate control loop and the bitstream formatting module. The inner loop, which dynamically adjusts the non-uniform quantizer step sizes, and the binary step size search uses most of the computational power.

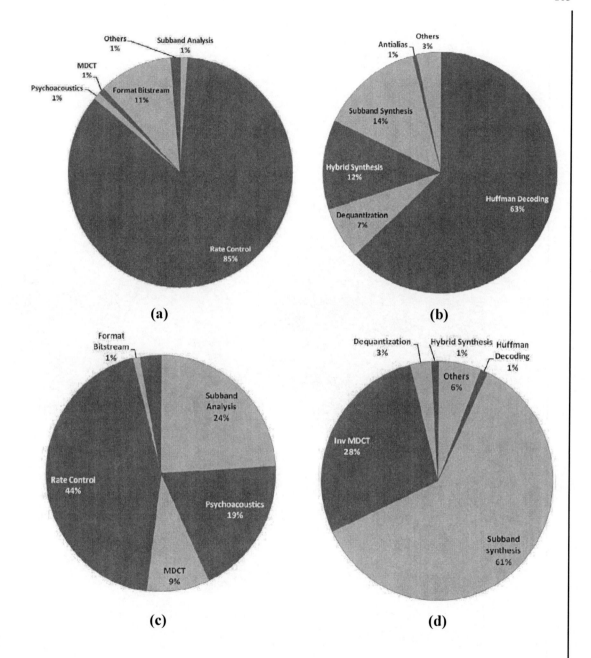

Figure A.2: Complexity Profile (a) Encoder implementation in MATLAB, (b) Decoder implementation in MATLAB, (c) ISO encoder implementation in C, (d) ISO decoder implementation in C.

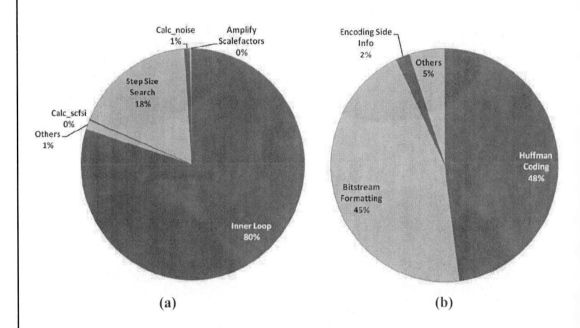

Figure A.3: Complexity Profile of the MATLAB implementation, (a) rate control module, (b) bitstream formatting.

Bibliography

[1] J. Blauert, Spatial Hearing. The MIT Press: Cambridge, MA, 1974. Cited on page(s) 1

[2] B. C. J. Moore and B. Glasberg, "Suggested Formulae for Calculating Auditory-Filter Bandwidths and Excitation Patterns," *J. Acous. Soc. Am.*, vol. 74, pp. 750–753, 1983. DOI: 10.1121/1.389861 Cited on page(s) 1

[3] B. C. J. Moore, "Masking in the Human Auditory System," in *Collected Papers on Digital Audio Bit-Rate Reduction*, N. Gilchrist and C. Grewin, Eds., Aud. Eng. Soc., pp. 9–19, 1996. Cited on page(s) 1

[4] B.C.J. Moore, An Introduction to the Psychology of Hearing, Academic Press, Fifth Edition, Jan. 2003. Cited on page(s) 1

[5] R. E. Crochiere, et al., "Digital Coding of Speech in Sub-Bands," *Bell Sys. Tech. J.*, vol. 55, n. 8, pp. 1069–1085, Oct. 1976. DOI: 10.1109/ICASSP.1976.1170079 Cited on page(s) 1

[6] M. A. Krasner, "Digital Encoding of Speech and Audio Signals based on the Perceptual Requirements of the Auditory System," *Technical Report* #535 of the MIT Lincoln Laboratory, Lexington 1979. Cited on page(s) 1

[7] H. J. Nussbaumer, "Pseudo QMF Filter Bank," *IBM Tech. Disclosure Bulletin*, vol. 24, pp. 3081–3087, Nov. 1981. Cited on page(s) 1, 22

[8] D. Krahe, "New Source Coding Method for High Quality Digital Audio Signals," *NTG Fachtagung Hoerrundfunk*, Mannheim, 1985. Cited on page(s) 1

[9] E. Schroder, and W. Voessing, "High Quality Digital Audio Encoding with 3.0 Bits/Sample using Adaptive Transform Coding," *Proc. 80th Conv. Audio Eng. Soc.*, preprint #2321, Mar. 1986. Cited on page(s) 1

[10] G. Theile, et al., "Low-Bit Rate Coding of High Quality Audio Signals," *Proc. 82nd Conv. Aud. Eng. Soc.*, preprint #2432, Mar. 1987. Cited on page(s) 1

[11] DTS-HD Master Audio, Available at http://www.dts.com/DTS_Audio_Formats/DTS-HD_Master_Audio.aspx. Cited on page(s) 1, 3

[12] MPEG-4 Audio Lossless Coddec, Available at http://www.nue.tu-berlin.de/menue/forschung/projekte/beendete_projekte/mpeg-4_audio_lossless_coding_als/parameter/en/. Cited on page(s) 1, 4

[13] Windows Media Audio 9 Lossless Codec, Available at `http://msdn.microsoft.com/en-us/library/ff819508(v=VS.85).aspx`. Cited on page(s) 1, 3

[14] K. Brandenburg, "OCF - A New Coding Algorithm for High Quality Sound Signals," *Proc. IEEE ICASSP-87*, pp. 5.1.1–5.1.4, May 1987. DOI: 10.1109/ICASSP.1987.1169893 Cited on page(s) 1

[15] J. Johnston, "Perceptual Transform Coding of Wideband Stereo Signals," *Proc. IEEE ICASSP-89*, pp. 1993–1996, May 1989. DOI: 10.1109/ICASSP.1989.266849 Cited on page(s) 1

[16] D. Sinha and A. Tewfik, "Low Bit Rate Transparent Audio Compression Using Adapted Wavelets," *IEEE Trans. Sig. Proc.*, pp. 3463–3479, Dec. 1993. DOI: 10.1109/78.258086 Cited on page(s) 1

[17] S. Boland and M. Deriche, "High Quality Audio Coding Using Multipulse LPC and Wavelet Decomposition," *Proc. IEEE ICASSP-95*, pp. 3067–3069, May 1995. DOI: 10.1109/ICASSP.1995.479493 Cited on page(s) 1

[18] K. Hamdy, *et al.*, "Low Bit Rate High Quality Audio Coding with Combined Harmonic and Wavelet Representations," in *Proc. IEEE ICASSP-96*, pp. 1045–1048, May 1996. DOI: 10.1109/ICASSP.1996.543542 Cited on page(s) 1

[19] K. Brandenburg and J. Johnston, "Second Generation Perceptual Audio Coding: The Hybrid Coder," *Proc. 88th Conv. Aud. Eng. Soc.*, preprint #2937, Mar. 1990. Cited on page(s) 1

[20] Y.F. Dehery, et al. (1991), "A MUSICAM Source Codec for Digital Audio Broadcasting and Storage," *Proc. IEEE ICASSP-91*, pp. 3605–3608, May 1991. DOI: 10.1109/ICASSP.1991.151054 Cited on page(s) 1

[21] M. Davis, "The AC-3 Multichannel Coder," *Proc. 95th Conv. Aud. Eng. Soc.*, preprint #3774, Oct. 1993. Cited on page(s) 1, 2

[22] J. Princen and J. Johnston, "Audio Coding with Signal Adaptive Filterbanks," *Proc. IEEE ICASSP-95*, pp. 3071–3074, May 1995. DOI: 10.1109/ICASSP.1995.479494 Cited on page(s) 1

[23] D. Sinha and J. Johnston, "Audio Compression at Low Bit Rates Using a Signal Adaptive Switched Filterbank," in *Proc. IEEE ICASSP-96*, pp. 1053–1056, May 1996. DOI: 10.1109/ICASSP.1996.543544 Cited on page(s) 1, 2

[24] W-Y Chan and A. Gersho, "High Fidelity Audio Transform Coding with Vector Quantization," *Proc. IEEE ICASSP-90*, pp. 1109–1112, May 1990. DOI: 10.1109/ICASSP.1990.116130 Cited on page(s) 1

[25] N. Iwakami, *et al.*, "High-Quality Audio-Coding at Less Than 64 kbit/s by Using Transform-Domain Weighted Interleave Vector Quantization (TWINVQ)," *Proc. IEEE ICASSP-95*, pp. 3095–3098, May. 1995. DOI: 10.1109/ICASSP.1995.479500 Cited on page(s) 1

[26] D. Wiese and G. Stoll, "Bitrate Reduction of High Quality Audio Signals by Modeling the Ear's Masking Thresholds," *Proc. 89th Conv. Aud. Eng. Soc.*, preprint #2970, Sep. 1990. Cited on page(s) 1

[27] ISO/IEC JTC1/SC29/WG11 MPEG, IS11172–3 "Information Technology - Coding of Moving Pictures and Associated Audio for Digital Storage Media at up to About 1.5 Mbit/s, Part 3: Audio" 1992. ("MPEG-1"). Cited on page(s) 2, 13, 25, 46, 53, 57, 75, 80

[28] ISO/IEC JTC1/SC29/WG11 MPEG, IS13818–3 "Information Technology - Generic Coding of Moving Pictures and Associated Audio, Part 3: Audio" 1994. ("MPEG-2 BC-LSF"). Cited on page(s) 2

[29] G.C.P. Lokhoff, "Precision adaptive sub-band coding (PASC) for the digital compact cassette (DCC)," *IEEE Trans. Consumer Electronics*, pp. 784–789, Nov. 1992. DOI: 10.1109/30.179966 Cited on page(s) 2

[30] J. Johnston, *et al.*, "AT&T Perceptual Audio Coding (PAC)," *in Collected Papers on Digital Audio Bit-Rate Reduction*, N. Gilchrist and C. Grewin, Eds., *Aud. Eng. Soc.*, pp. 73–81, 1996. Cited on page(s) 2

[31] G. Davidson and M. Bosi, "AC-2: High Quality Audio Coding for Broadcasting and Storage," *Proc. 46th Annual Broadcast Eng. Conf.*, pp. 98–105, Apr. 1992. Cited on page(s) 2

[32] L. Fielder and G. Davidson, "AC-2: A Family of Low Complexity Transform-Based Music Coders," *Proc. 10th Conv. Aud. Eng. Soc.*, Sep. 1991. Cited on page(s) 2

[33] L. Fielder, *et al.*, "AC-2 and AC-3: Low-Complexity Transform-Based Audio Coding," *in Collected Papers on Digital Audio Bit-Rate Reduction*, N. Gilchrist and C. Grewin, Eds., *Aud. Eng. Soc.*, pp. 54–72, 1996. Cited on page(s) 2

[34] T. Yoshida, "The Rewritable MiniDisc System," *Proc. IEEE*, pp. 1492–1500, Oct. 1994. DOI: 10.1109/5.326407 Cited on page(s) 2

[35] K. Tsutsui, *et al.*, "ATRAC: Adaptive Transform Acoustic Coding for MiniDisc," *in Collected Papers on Digital Audio Bit-Rate Reduction*, N. Gilchrist and C. Grewin, Eds., Aud. Eng. Soc., pp. 95–101, 1996. Cited on page(s) 2

[36] T. Robinson, "SHORTEN: Simple lossless and near-lossless waveform compression," *Technical Report 156*, Engineering Department, Cambridge University, Dec. 1994. Cited on page(s) 2

[37] F. Wylie, "apt-X100: Low-Delay, Low-Bit-Rate-Subband ADPCM Digital Audio Coding," *in Collected Papers on Digital Audio Bit-Rate Reduction*, N. Gilchrist and C. Grewin, Eds., Aud. Eng. Soc., pp. 83–94, 1996. Cited on page(s) 2

[38] ISO/IEC JTC1/SC29/WG11 MPEG, Committee Draft 13818–7 "Generic Coding of Moving Pictures and Associated Audio: Audio (non backwards compatible coding, NBC)" 1996. ("MPEG-2 NBC/AAC"). Cited on page(s) 2

[39] M. Smyth, "White paper: An overview of the coherent acoustics coding system," June 1999 (available on the Internet – DTS web-page). Cited on page(s) 2

[40] P. G. Craven, M. Law, and J. Stuart, "Lossless compression using IIR prediction filters," *Proc. 102nd Conv. Aud. Eng. Soc.*, Munich, preprint #4415, March, 1997. Cited on page(s)

[41] A. Wegener, "MUSICompress: Lossless, Low-MIPS Audio Compression in Software and Hardware," in *Proc. of the International Conference on Signal Processing Applications and Technology*, Sept. 1997. Cited on page(s) 2

[42] M. Purat, T. Liebchen, and P. Noll, "Lossless Transform Coding of Audio Signals," *Proc. 102nd Conv. Audio Eng. Soc.*, preprint #4414, March, 1997. Cited on page(s) 2

[43] M. Hans and R. W. Schafer, "AudioPaK – An integer arithmetic lossless audio codec," in *Proc. Data Compression Conf.* Snowbird, UT, 1998, p.550. DOI: 10.1109/DCC.1998.672286 Cited on page(s)

[44] M. Hans and R. W. Schafer, "Lossless compression of digital audio," in *IEEE Sig. Proc. Mag.*, July 2001. DOI: 10.1109/79.939834 Cited on page(s) 2

[45] ISO/IEC JTC1/SC29/WG11 (MPEG), International Standard ISO/IEC 14496–3: "Coding of Audio-Visual Objects – Part 3: Audio," 1999. ("MPEG-4"). Cited on page(s) 2

[46] M. A. Gerzon, J. R. Stuart, R. J. Wilson, P. G. Craven, and M. J. Law, "The MLP Lossless Compression System," in *AES 17th Int. Conf. High-Quality Audio Coding*, Florence, Italy, Sept. 1999, pp. 61–75. Cited on page(s) 2, 3

[47] ISO/IEC JTC1/SC29/WG11 (MPEG), International Standard ISO/IEC 14496–3 AMD-1: "Coding of Audio-Visual Objects – Part 3: Audio," 2000. ("MPEG-4 version-2"). Cited on page(s) 2

[48] ISO/IEC JTC1/SC29/WG11 MPEG, IS15938–4 "Multimedia Content Description Interface: Audio," International Standard, Sept. 2001. ("MPEG-7: Part-4"). Cited on page(s) 2, 3

[49] R. Geiger, T. Sporer, J. Koller, and K. Brandenburg, "Audio coding based on integer transforms," in *Proc. 111th Conv. Aud. Eng. Soc.*, New York, 2001. Cited on page(s) 2

[50] R. Geiger, J. Herre, J. Koller, and K. Brandenburg, "IntMDCT – A link between perceptual and lossless audio coding," *Proc. IEEE ICASSP-2002*, vol.2, pp. 1813–1816, May 2002.
DOI: 10.1109/ICASSP.2002.5744976 Cited on page(s) 2

[51] D. Reefman and E. Janssen, "White paper on signal processing for SACD," Philips IP&S,
[Online] Available: `http://www.superaudiocd.philips.com`, clickDOWNLOADS. Cited
on page(s) 2, 3

[52] E. Janssen and D. Reefman, "Super-Audio CD: An Introduction," in *IEEE Sig. Proc. Mag.*,
pp. 83–90, July 2003. DOI: 10.1109/MSP.2003.1226728 Cited on page(s) 2

[53] MPEG Requirements Group, MPEG-21 Overview, ISO/MPEG N5231, Oct. 2002. Cited
on page(s) 2, 3

[54] T. Holman, "New factors in sound for cinema and television," in *J. Audio Eng. Soc.*, Vol. 39,
pp. 529–539, July-August 1999. Cited on page(s) 2

[55] M. Bosi, et al, "Aspects of current standardization activities for high-quality low rate multi-
channel audio coding," *Proc. of IEEE Workshop on App. of Sig. Proc. to Audio and Acoustics*, New
Paltz, New York, Oct 1993. DOI: 10.1109/ASPAA.1993.379999 Cited on page(s) 2

[56] M. Bosi, "High-quality multichannel audio coding: Trends and Challenges," *J. Audio Eng. Soc.*,
Vol. 48, No. 6, pp.588, 2000. Cited on page(s) 2

[57] R. Koenen, "Overview of the MPEG-4 Standard," ISO/IEC JTC1/SC29/WG11 N2323,
Jul. 1998. (`http://www.cselt.it/mpeg/standards/mpeg-4/mpeg-4.html`.) Cited on
page(s) 2

[58] R. Koenen, "Overview of the MPEG-4 Standard," ISO/IEC JTC1/SC29/WG11 N3156,
Dec. 1999. (`http://www.cselt.it/mpeg/standards/mpeg-4/mpeg-4.htm`.) Cited on
page(s) 2

[59] E. Allamanche, R. Geiger, J. Herre, Th. Sporer, "MPEG-4 Low Delay Audio Coding Based
on the AAC Codec," *107th AES Convention*, Munich 1999. Cited on page(s) 2

[60] S. Wabnik, G. Schuller, J. Hirschfeld and U. Kramer, "Reduced Bit Rate Ultra Low Delay
Audio Coding," *120th AES Convention*, May 2006, Paris, France. Cited on page(s) 2

[61] U. Kramer, G. Schuller, S. Wabnik, J. Klier, J. Hirschfeld and, "Ultra Low Delay Audio Coding
with Constant Bit Rate," *117th AES Convention*, Oct 2004, San Francisco. Cited on page(s) 2

[62] ISO/IEC JTC1/SC29/WG11 MPEG, "MPEG-7 Applications Document," Doc. N3934,
Jan. 2001. (Also available on-line: `http://www.cselt.it/mpeg`.) Cited on page(s) 3

[63] Sony Adaptive Transform Acoustic Coding. Available at `http://www.sony.net/`
`Products/ATRAC3/`. Cited on page(s) 3

[64] H. Purnhagen and N. Meine, "HILN-the MPEG-4 parametric audio coding tools," *Proceedings of ISCAS 2000 Genev*, vol.3, no., pp.201–204 vol.3, 2000. DOI: 10.1109/ISCAS.2000.856031 Cited on page(s) 3

[65] P. G. Craven and M. Gerzon, "Lossless coding for Audio Discs," *J. Audio Eng. Soc.*, Vol. 44, no.9, pp. 706–720, Sept. 1996. Cited on page(s) 3

[66] Apple Lossless Audio Codec, Available at http://www.apple.com/itunes/features/#importing. Cited on page(s) 3

[67] Dolby TrueHD, Available at http://www.dolby.com/consumer/understand/playback/dolby-truehd.html. Cited on page(s) 3

[68] "DTS-HD Audio: Consumer White Paper for Blu-ray Disc and HD DVD Applications", November 2006. Cited on page(s) 4

[69] T. Cover and J. Thomas, *Elements of Information Theory*. John Wiley and Sons, Inc.: New York, 1991. Cited on page(s) 5

[70] I. Witten, "Arithmetic Coding for Data Compression," *Comm. ACM*, vol. 30, n. 6, pp. 520–540, Jun. 1987. DOI: 10.1145/214762.214771 Cited on page(s) 5

[71] J. Ziv and A. Lempel, "A Universal Algorithm for Sequential Data Compression," *IEEE Trans. on Info. Theory*, vol. IT-23, n. 3, pp. 337–343, May 1977. DOI: 10.1109/TIT.1977.1055714 Cited on page(s) 5

[72] A. Spanias, T. Painter and V. Atti, Audio signal processing and coding. Wiley-Interscience, John Wiley & Sons, Sep. 2007. Cited on page(s) 6, 7, 8, 9, 11, 13, 46

[73] T. Painter and A. Spanias, "Perceptual coding of digital audio," *Proceedings of the IEEE*, vol.88, no.4, pp.451–515, Apr 2000. DOI: 10.1109/5.842996 Cited on page(s) 13, 14, 25, 40, 58

[74] P. P. Vaidyanathan, "Quadrature mirror filter banks, M-band extensions, and perfect-reconstruction techniques," *IEEE Acoust., Speech, Signal Processing Mag.*, pp. 4–20, Jul. 1987. DOI: 10.1109/MASSP.1987.1165589 Cited on page(s) 13

[75] P. P. Vaidyanathan, "Multirate digital filters, filter banks, polyphase networks, and applications: A tutorial," *Proc. IEEE*, vol. 78, pp. 56–93, Jan. 1990. DOI: 10.1109/5.52200 Cited on page(s) 13

[76] J. Johnston, S. Quackenbush, G. Davidson, K. Brandenburg, and J. Herre, "MPEG audio coding," in *Wavelet, Subband, and Block Transforms in Communications and Multimedia*, A. Akansu and M. Medley, Eds. Boston, MA: Kluwer Academic, 1999, ch. 7. Cited on page(s) 13

[77] R. E. Crochiere and L. R. Rabiner, Multirate Digital Signal Processing. Englewood Cliffs, NJ: Prentice-Hall, 1983. Cited on page(s) 13

[78] S. Shlien, "Guide to MPEG-1 audio standard," *IEEE Trans. Broadcast.*, pp. 206–218, Dec. 1994. DOI: 10.1109/11.362938 Cited on page(s) 22, 99

[79] P. P. Vaidyanathan, Multirate Systems and Filter Banks. Englewood Cliffs, NJ: Prentice-Hall, 1993. Cited on page(s) 22

[80] A. Akansu and M. J. T. Smith, Eds., Subband and Wavelet Transforms, Design and Applications. Norwell, MA: Kluwer Academic, 1996. Cited on page(s) 22

[81] H. S. Malvar, Signal Processing with Lapped Transforms. Norwood, MA: Artech House, 1991. Cited on page(s) 22

[82] K. Brandenburg, E. Eberlein, J. Herre, and B. Edler, "Comparison of filter banks for high quality audio coding," in *Proc. IEEE ISCAS*, 1992, pp. 1336–1339.
DOI: 10.1109/ISCAS.1992.230257 Cited on page(s) 22

[83] J. H. Rothweiler, "Polyphase quadrature filters: A new subband coding technique," in *Proc. Int. Conf. Acoustics, Speech, and Signal Processing (ICASSP-83)*, May 1983, pp. 1280–1283. DOI: 10.1109/ICASSP.1983.1172005 Cited on page(s) 22

[84] T. Ramstad, "Cosine modulated analysis–synthesis filter bank with critical sampling and perfect reconstruction," in *Proc. Int. Conf. Acoustics, Speech, and Signal Processing (ICASSP-91)*, May 1991, pp. 1789–1792. DOI: 10.1109/ICASSP.1991.150684 Cited on page(s) 22

[85] H. Malvar, "Lapped transforms for efficient transform/subband coding," *IEEE Trans. Acoust., Speech, Signal Processing*, vol. 38, pp. 969–978, June 1990. DOI: 10.1109/29.56057 Cited on page(s) 22

[86] J. Johnston, "Transform Coding of Audio Signals Using Perceptual Noise Criteria," *IEEE J. Sel. Areas in Comm.*, pp. 314–323, Feb. 1988. DOI: 10.1109/49.608 Cited on page(s) 25, 42, 46

[87] J. Johnston, "Estimation of Perceptual Entropy Using Noise Masking Criteria," *Proc. IEEE ICASSP-88*, pp. 2524–2527, May 1988. DOI: 10.1109/ICASSP.1988.197157 Cited on page(s) 25

[88] E. Zwicker and H. Fastl, Psychoacoustics Facts and Models. Berlin, Germany: Springer-Verlag, 1990. Cited on page(s) 25, 40, 46

[89] D. Pan, "A Tutorial on MPEG/Audio Compression", *IEEE Multimedia*, vol.2, no.2, pp.60–74, 1995. DOI: 10.1109/93.388209 Cited on page(s) 27, 80

[90] B. Scharf, "Critical bands," in *Foundations of Modern Auditory Theory*. New York: Academic, 1970. Cited on page(s) 28

[91] R. Hellman, "Asymmetry of masking between noise and tone," *Percep. Psychphys.*, vol. 11, pp. 241–246, 1972. DOI: 10.3758/BF03206257 Cited on page(s) 28

[92] J. L. Hall, "Auditory psychophysics for coding applications," in *The Digital Signal Processing Handbook*, V. Madisetti and D.Williams, Eds. Boca Raton, FL: CRC Press, 1998, pp. 39.1–39.25. Cited on page(s) 29

[93] P. Noll, "Wideband speech and audio coding," *IEEE Commun. Mag.*, pp. 34–44, Nov. 1993. DOI: 10.1109/35.256878 Cited on page(s) 31, 58

[94] N. Jayant, J. D. Johnston, and R. Safranek, "Signal compression based on models of human perception," *Proc. IEEE*, vol. 81, pp. 1385–1422, Oct. 1993. DOI: 10.1109/5.241504 Cited on page(s) 31, 46

[95] M. Schroeder, B. S. Atal, and J. L. Hall, "Optimizing digital speech coders by exploiting masking properties of the human ear," *J. Acoust. Soc. Amer.*, pp. 1647–1652, Dec. 1979. DOI: 10.1121/1.383662 Cited on page(s) 31

[96] B. C. J. Moore, "Masking in the human auditory system," in *Collected Papers on Digital Audio Bit-Rate Reduction*, N. Gilchrist and C. Grewin, Eds., 1996, pp. 9–19. Cited on page(s) 35

[97] K. Brandenburg, "Perceptual coding of high quality digital audio," in *Applications of Digital Signal Processing to Audio and Acoustics*,M. Kahrs and K. Brandenburg, Eds. Boston, MA: Kluwer Academic,1998. Cited on page(s) 36

[98] P. Papamichalis, "MPEG audio compression: Algorithms and implementation," in *Proc. DSP 95 Int. Conf. DSP*, June 1995, pp. 72–77. Cited on page(s) 36

[99] H. Fletcher, "Auditory patterns," *Rev. Mod. Phys.*, pp. 47–65, Jan.1940. DOI: 10.1103/RevModPhys.12.47 Cited on page(s) 39

[100] E. Terhardt, "Calculating virtual pitch," *Hearing Res.*, vol. 1, pp.155–182, 1979. DOI: 10.1016/0378-5955(79)90025-X Cited on page(s) 39

[101] K. Tsutsui, "ATRAC (adaptive transform acoustic coding) and ATRAC 2," in *The Digital Signal Processing Handbook*, V. Madisetti and D. Williams, Eds. Boca Raton, FL: CRC Press, 1998, pp. 43.16–43.20. Cited on page(s) 42

[102] J. Johnston, D. Sinha, S. Dorward, and S. Quackenbush, "AT&T perceptual audio coding (PAC)," *Collected Papers on Digital Audio Bit-Rate Reduction*, pp. 73–81, 1996. Cited on page(s) 42, 75, 80

[103] D. Pan, "Digital audio compression," *Digital Tech. J.*, vol. 5, no. 2, pp. 28–40, 1993. Cited on page(s) 47, 80

[104] K. Konstantinides, "Fast subband filtering in MPEG audio coding," *IEEE Signal Processing Lett.*, vol. 1, pp. 26–28, Feb. 1994. DOI: 10.1109/97.300309 Cited on page(s) 47

[105] P. L. Chu, "Quadrature mirror filter design for an arbitrary number of equal bandwidth channels," *IEEE Trans. Acoust., Speech, Signal Processing*, vol. ASSP–33, pp. 203–218, Feb. 1985. DOI: 10.1109/TASSP.1985.1164529 Cited on page(s) 54

[106] J. Masson and Z. Picel, "Flexible design of computationally efficient nearly perfect QMF filter banks," in *Proc. Int. Conf. Acoustics, Speech, and Signal Processing (ICASSP-85)*, Mar. 1985, pp. 14.7.1–14.7.4. DOI: 10.1109/ICASSP.1985.1168361 Cited on page(s) 54

[107] R. Cox, "The design of uniformly and nonuniformly spaced pseudo QMF," *IEEE Trans. Acoust., Speech, Signal Processing*, vol. ASSP–34, pp. 1090–1096, Oct. 1986. DOI: 10.1109/TASSP.1986.1164945 Cited on page(s) 54

[108] R. Koilpillai and P. P. Vaidyanathan, "New results on cosine-modulated FIR filter banks satisfying perfect reconstruction," in *Proc. Int. Conf. Acoustics, Speech, and Signal Processing (ICASSP-91)*, May 1991, pp. 1793–1796. DOI: 10.1109/ICASSP.1991.150685 Cited on page(s) 54

[109] R. Koilpillai and P. P. Vaidyanathan, "Cosine-modulated FIR filter banks satisfying perfect reconstruction," *IEEE Trans. Signal Processing*, vol. SP–40, pp. 770–783, Apr. 1992. DOI: 10.1109/78.127951 Cited on page(s) 54

[110] J. Princen and A. Bradley, "Analysis/synthesis filter bank design based on time domain aliasing cancellation," *IEEE Trans. Acoust., Speech, Signal Processing*, vol. ASSP-34, pp. 1153–1161, Oct. 1986. DOI: 10.1109/TASSP.1986.1164954 Cited on page(s) 54

[111] G. Smart and A. Bradley, "Filter bank design based on time-domain aliasing cancellation with nonidentical windows," in *Proc. Int. Conf. Acoustics, Speech, and Signal Processing (ICASSP-94)*, May 1995, pp. III-185–III-188. DOI: 10.1109/ICASSP.1994.390059 Cited on page(s) 54

[112] M. Link, "An attack processing of audio signals for optimizing the temporal characteristics of a low bit-rate audio coding system," in *Proc. 95th Conv. Aud. Eng. Soc.*, 1993, preprint 3696. Cited on page(s) 75

[113] K. Akagiri, "Technical description of Sony preprocessing," SO/IEC JTC1/SC29/WG11 MPEGI, Input Doc., 1994. Cited on page(s) 75

[114] J. Herre and J. Johnston, "Enhancing the performance of perceptual audio coders by using temporal noise shaping (TNS)," in *Proc. 101st Conv. Aud. Eng. Soc.*, 1996, preprint 4384. Cited on page(s) 75

[115] M. Bosi, K. Brandenburg, S. Quackenbush, L. Fielder, K. Akagiri, H. Fuchs, and M. Dietz, "MPEG-2 advanced audio coding," in *Proc. 101st Conv. Aud. Eng. Soc.*, 1996, preprint. Cited on page(s) 75

[116] T. Uzelac, M. Kovac, "A fast MPEG audio layer III software decoder," *Southeastcon '98. Proceedings. IEEE* , pp.43–46, 24-26 Apr 1998. DOI: 10.1109/SECON.1998.673287 Cited on page(s) 97

[117] T. Tsai, T. Chen; L. Chen, "An MPEG audio decoder chip," *Consumer Electronics, IEEE Transactions on* , vol.41, no.1, pp.89–96, Feb 1995. DOI: 10.1109/30.370314 Cited on page(s) 97

[118] G. Maturi, "Single chip MPEG audio decoder," *Consumer Electronics.* DOI: 10.1109/30.156706 Cited on page(s) 97

Authors' Biographies

JAYARAMAN J. THIAGARAJAN

Jayaraman J. Thiagarajan completed his MS in Electrical Engineering and is currently a PhD candidate in the School of Electrical, Computer, and Energy Engineering at Arizona State University. His research interests are in the areas of DSP, audio processing and coding, sparse representations and computer vision. His works in sparse representations have been nominated for awards at IEEE DSP Workshop 2011 and Asilomar 2011. He has worked extensively with the MPEG-1 Layer-III audio coding standard and has created MATLAB modules for the various functions of the algorithm. In addition, he has developed LabVIEW interfaces for teaching speech coding algorithms and contributed to the Java-DSP software package.

ANDREAS SPANIAS

Andreas Spanias is a Professor in the School of Electrical, Computer, and Energy Engineering at Arizona State University (ASU). He is also the founder and director of the SenSIP Center and NSF NCSS I/UCRC site. His research interests are in the areas of adaptive signal processing, speech processing, and audio sensing. He and his student team developed the computer simulation software Java-DSP (JDSP– ISBN 0-9724984-0-0). He is author of two text books: *Audio Processing and Coding* by Wiley and *DSP: An Interactive Approach.* He served as Associate Editor of the IEEE Transactions on Signal Processing and as General Co-chair of IEEE ICASSP-99. He also served as the IEEE Signal Processing Vice-President for Conferences. Andreas Spanias is co-recipient of the 2002 IEEE Donald G. Fink paper prize award and was elected Fellow of the IEEE in 2003. He served as Distinguished lecturer for the IEEE Signal processing society in 2004.

Lightning Source UK Ltd.
Milton Keynes UK
UKOW042158160212

187407UK00001B/31/P